"THE GODS OF WAR"

Written by Ben Speed
Formally Capt. James B. Speed
U.S. Army

Table of Contents:

Introduction:

This book contains a series of stories about my tour in Vietnam and the years around that tour. Each story is true and told as it happened without embellishments or judgments added. Some of these stories were boring, so I left most of them out. Some were boring as a war story but interesting as a life story. I kept some of those.

We, helicopter pilots, had a saying about flying in Vietnam. We endured hours and hours of boredom, punctuated with moments of stark terror.

The boring war stories have been left out. They were as boring for me to write as they would have been for you to read. Most of what I write about will be those "moments of terror" that we hear so much about. Everyone loves a good war story, right? No one ever asked a veteran to tell them a boring story.

Therein lies the bed of thorns. We go to movies and expect to be entertained by war stories. We want to come out of the theater feeling good about America and its warriors. It gives us a sense of pride to know that because we are Americans, God is on our side. We pay to see our actors overcome the odds and come home heroes. After all, they portray our young men and women in the armed forces. We expect our veterans to do the same. We Americans crave excitement and vicarious glory.

Have you ever noticed that most Korean and Vietnam veterans rarely tell war stories? A good percentage of the ones that do are lying. I contend that most of the guys who brag about their Vietnam escapades were company clerks. Desk jockeys.

There's a reason for that. We call our World War II veterans the greatest generation. I doubt you have heard those words about war after 1945. World War II was a war to save the world from tyranny. We lost many great men fighting those battles. But they came home winners. Those men saved the world.

I must have saved a crapload of something. But for the life of me, I can't tell you why we were in Vietnam or what we were fighting for. Before I went, I thought that I knew. When I came back home, I wasn't sure. There weren't any parades or newscasts about our bravery. Most of what I saw were demonstrations wanting the war in Vietnam to end. After a while, I was ashamed to admit that I was there.

I want this book to take you into the cinema and let you peek behind the curtains and see real life taking place. I would like you to see what being a warrior is really like. This book will help you realize just how little glory there is in war. There is bravery and valor for sure, but very little glory. I hope this book will help people who have never seen the carnage of a battlefield realize just how little glory there is when the cameras aren't filming.

**Before you start reading, I would like you to know something. I'm dyslexic. I've only once tried to read a book cover to cover. Five minutes after I set it down, I couldn't remember the main character's name or the storyline. The only way I can write my books is with the help of aids. I have the "Read Aloud" program on my computer. It lets me hear what I am writing before I publish. I use Grammarly and Google Docs to help. My wife and sister help edit what I write.

But, as many times as we check, there are always errors left. I apologize. I'm not ignorant. I have a high I.Q. Most people, but not all, who are dyslexic have above-average I.Q.s. Most, but not all.

I write in a less formal style. I write more as people speak. If you have problems reading this book, read it out loud. Trust me, it works. This is the twelfth book I've written. I'm working on developing a more formal written word, but I'm not there yet.

(One of my buddies is dyslexic and doesn't have a clue what I'm talking about. He says it's the first book he's ever read that he understood..... I am sorry about that.)

Chapter 1: Old People

I'm not sure how to say this except to say it. I'm getting old... no, that's not right. I'm old. I'm getting old enough that I need to start writing some of this stuff down before I forget the facts and need to fill in the blanks in my memories with things I make up. That happens to everyone as they age, but some people do it more often than they should. They find themselves getting left behind and looking for ways to become relevant again. They can't stand on their heads or do fifty push-ups, so they start embellishing their stories just a little. If that works, they begin changing the rest of their stories, making them sound more interesting. Or, in some cases, they start filling in forgotten parts of their stories with new facts. Who knows? Don't misunderstand. I'm not making excuses for old people. I'm one of them.

From where I sit, everything is still the same as it has always been. I see people around me getting older, and I know I must be getting older, too, but I don't see it happening. So, I don't think about it. I see all these old farts around me getting old, but that's as far as it goes. I'm like the ostrich sticking my head in the sand.

 Sure, there are the odd times when I saw a photograph of myself when I was younger. I recognize my younger self, but I live inside my skin every day. I know that inside, I'm still myself. I'm like the farmer who puts on a suit. Inside, he knows that he is still a farmer. He doesn't lose his identity just because some things around him change.

From the inside out, everything is still the same as it has always been. I'm still me. I've looked at myself in the mirror at least once every day. If I've changed, it happened so slowly that I didn't notice.

It's not just me. If you want to have fun at an old person's expense, it's easy. I'll give you a perfect example. A couple of weeks ago, one of my neighbors told my wife and me, "How cute we looked riding our Schwinn bicycles around the neighborhood." So cute? She could have said that my hair was on fire, and I wouldn't have been as shocked as I was hearing her say that. I might have considered handsome a compliment, maybe, but cute?

I'm old, and old people spend a lot of time ruminating about old times. Sometimes, we talk more about what could have been or should have been when we should be talking about what was. I made up my mind that I wouldn't do that while writing this book. Watering down my stories with "what ifs" isn't practical. I don't have that much ink in my printer. Besides, it's annoying.

If there is one thing I can say about my life with any degree of certainty, it sure as hell hasn't been boring. As early as I can remember, I was one of those people that craved and looked for adventure. Not the kind of adventure that would get me in trouble or put my life in danger. The kind that kept things interesting. I learned soon enough that nature would provide dangerous adventures without my help.

I've written eleven novels. I've proven that I can write fiction anytime I choose. Writing the truth is a more difficult task. I've been working on this one for ten years or more.

One last warning. Listening to old people tell stories is like spitting into a hot frying pan. Both bounce around without any hint of where they're going next. Some people, mostly younger people, think it is because old people find it difficult to choose their words. This isn't true. Old people slow their speech down because they understand the power of words. They spend more time choosing their words because they know they have power. They want to be sure that the words they choose accurately express how they feel. But even more important, they take the extra time to choose words based on how those words will make you feel. That's the real secret of words. Most, but not all, older people have learned that words carry consequences. Therefore, they try to avoid misallocating frivolously used words.

Here we go; there will be those who say there cannot be a misallocation of words. They will say that allocation refers to money or funds, not words. To those misinformed people, I would like to point out that you paid funds for these words, didn't you?

My Story in No Particular Order
Chapter 2: Wanderlust

The year was 1970; maybe '71, I'm not sure which. In those days, time didn't seem as important as now.

When you're young, you don't keep track of time the same as you will later. Young people, especially during the early 70s, lived more in the moment than they do today. But none of that matters here. It doesn't have anything to do with my story.

1970, John Johnson and I decided we wanted to ride horseback over Guanella Pass in Colorado and on to Mexico. (It was John's idea. I was along for the ride.) John believed that National Geographic would want to film our trip after we were out for a while.

I didn't.

To pay for this adventure, John introduced me to hard-rock mining. Late in 1970, we took jobs as muckers in the Schwartzwalder Uranium mine somewhere up Golden Gate Canyon between Golden and Central City, more or less. Jefferson County is close enough for this story. John and I worked in the mine for four months, making eleven dollars in hourly wages and another eleven dollars an hour in bonuses. Twenty-two dollars an hour, eight hours a day, five days a week. That works out to somewhere around eight hundred and eighty dollars a week. Or about four grand a month before taxes. To put that in perspective, the average yearly income in 1971 was $10,383.00. We were being well paid.

I was issued an eight-pound "double jack" (sledgehammer), a safety helmet with a light attached, a belt to hold the battery, wading boots, a pair of rubber waders, and one pair of gloves. My first day in the mine started when I stepped into the "bucket" and was lowered into the abyss. I started on the third level.

My job was to come in behind the miners and clean up after they set off charges. By clean up, I mean I took big rocks, broke them into smaller rocks, and loaded them in my cart. Then, I pushed that cart down the track to the dump.

For safety's sake, we worked in pairs. We were expected to fill a minimum of twenty-five carts per shift. A cart usually held one ton, depending on how full you filled it. You could light load if you wanted, but you still needed to clean out the tunnel before the miners returned to start the process over.

Did I mention that this was a hard-rock mine? Solid rock.

We were doing thirty to thirty-five tons a shift. The next shift was expected to finish cleaning up and have the tunnel ready for the day crew.

One night my partner was a no-show, and my straw boss told me I could go home if I wanted. He didn't have anyone to put with me. I talked him into letting me work alone. I did forty-two tons by myself. The next night, I was moved down to the fifth level and put on the two-ton cart by myself. It was the best job that I ever had. Nobody screwed with me if I did my job. To be sure, I always did a little extra.

A few side notes: The only light in a mine comes from the lamp on a miner's helmet. If you turn off your lamp, you can't see your hand in front of your face. That's when I learned what pitch black meant. No sounds could be heard except those you created. I've never felt as comfortable as when

I took my thirty-minute lunch break, turned off my lamp, and sat in the dark eating.

One night, my straw boss showed me a "room" in the mine that was so large that the beam from my lamp would not shine far enough to see from one side to the other or from the floor to the ceiling. I wish I could remember what he called it. Maybe the Michigan room or something like that. It looked large enough to hold Mile High Stadium and have space left to spare.

In the four months I worked there, I went from 225 pounds and a 39-inch waist to 225 pounds and a 33-inch waist. I could crack walnuts between my thumb and index finger.

Sometime in April, John decided that we had enough money to pay for our trip over Guanella Pass and on to parts unknown, and we cashed in. We spent the next month buying five horses, saddles, tents, and supplies and getting acquainted with our horses. Once your horse gets used to your quirks, he prefers you to be his rider. Only you. That bond between a man and his horse feels good.

April turned into May, and we decided it was time to head out. We started our journey by crossing over Virginia Canyon Pass between Central City and Idaho Springs. We might have made six miles on our first day.

We woke up at daybreak only to find that our horses were gone. They had been hobbled the night before, so our first job was to figure out their direction, track them down, and bring them back to our camp. My horse was the largest and the most hard-headed. His usual routine was to return to the barn whenever we stopped. We found them about two miles back over the pass and headed back to Central City. How they went two miles hobbled is still a mystery. (Hobbles and handcuffs are similar.) It took two days to go the first twenty-some-odd miles. We started our third day camped at the base of Guanella Pass in Empire.

Day three was uneventful. It was early May, so it was cold at night. Nevertheless, we made the best of it, built a campfire, and cooked our first meal. Before that, we were eating the meals that we had brought along. We were tired, and our butts were sore, so we went to bed in our tents early.

The following morning was probably the warmest since we left Central City. It snowed that night. It took twenty minutes to dig my way out of my tent. Our horses were tied under a group of trees for protection from the weather. They had snow on their backs and ice sickles hanging from their stomach to the ground. There had been a spring snowstorm... no, if I remember right, the news stations on the radio were calling it a blizzard. It took all day to get down off the side of that mountain. At the bottom of the pass, we were met by a rescue team, John's father, and a veterinarian. I'm not sure if John's father brought the vet or if he was part of the rescue team. He insisted that our horses have shots before he turned us over to our unneeded rescue team. We made the nightly news.

After that, we needed a break, so we decided to hitchhike from Central City, Colorado, to Pensacola, Florida. My thinking at the time had something to do with the weather in Florida. In Pensacola, people were going to the beaches. They were still snow skiing in Colorado.

Our challenge was to do it without taking any money. John said that we were less likely to be robbed. I didn't point out the obvious flaw in his theory. I should have. It proved to be a problem each time we were hungry.

Two days later, John and I walked down to Black Hawk and stuck out our thumbs. Luck was on our side. We caught a flatlander on his way home from Central City back to Denver. Our first ride took us down to Denver, where I-25 and I-70 cross. We had to catch a ride before the Highway Patrol caught us. It was illegal to hitchhike on the Interstate back then.

Our luck held out. A nearly new Impala convertible pulled over within a half-hour, and we jumped in. The driver was maybe in her early forties. We were in our mid-twenties. She smiled and immediately reached under her seat and pulled out a bottle of vodka. We passed. Even at our age, we knew that driving and drinking weren't smart. Her next offer was even more direct. Neither John nor I were into threesomes, so again, we passed. She stopped somewhere between Colorado Springs and Pueblo and asked us to get out. That was the end of our luck.

It took almost the rest of the day to catch a ride to the Highway 50 exit. Then, it took another two hours to catch our next one. It was the most interesting, no, make that our second most interesting ride of the trip.

John and I sat on our bags and waited until late in the evening before our next ride stopped. It was an eighteen-wheel semi, cattle truck, running empty. Drivers usually pass a hitchhiker so that they get a good look at them before they stop. That usually results in a quarter-mile run before you get in. However, this semi started slowing down at least a mile before he got to us. Finally, he came to a complete stop when his passenger window was directly above us. We weren't brave enough to jump up and stick our heads inside without knowing who was waiting, so we just stood there and waited.

Finally, the driver stuck his head out of the passenger window. He asked if either of us had a license to drive a rig like his. John did. I didn't. He told John to get in. Just John. To John's credit, he said no. The guy thought about it for a minute and then said that we could both get in, and he crawled into the sleeper.

John couldn't drive a semi. He had a CDL but used it to drive an old hay truck. That didn't stop John. He asked the guy to show him the gear pattern. The driver looked at John funny but showed him and then told John that we were going to Abilene, Texas. Five minutes later, he was snoring. He slept for the next five hours.

John finally had to wake the guy and tell him we were running low on fuel. After we all got out and pissed, I expected him to drive off and leave John and me at that truck stop. He didn't. He bought each of us hamburgers, fries, and a drink and told us his story. As it turned out, he did need someone... anyone else, to drive.

He told us he was on his third day without sleep when he picked us up. I'll paraphrase what he said. "I was bouncing bennies off the windshield into my mouth, trying to stay awake. Then, as I started coming out of the mountains, I saw a tunnel ahead. I realized that I wasn't going to clear it. So I slammed on my brakes and almost lost control of my rig. I ended up jack-knifed in the middle of I-25. I had traffic stopped in both directions. When I got out to see if I was stuck under the entrance of that tunnel, I looked around and realized that I was in the middle of a desert. So I stopped and picked you guys up right after that."

I'm not sure which mountains he was coming down from. Maybe outside of Colorado Springs, but I doubt it. More than likely, he was confused, and it was I-70 coming into Denver. As far as any desert? I think he was near Pueblo. Of course, that's just guessing on my part. Long story made short. He was stoned out of his gourd from the lack of sleep and the bennies.

He dropped us off just past Abilene, Texas. He warned us that we shouldn't wait too long before catching our next ride. "Cowboys don't like hippies with beards." We tried to explain that almost all miners had beards. It protected their faces from rock chips. He laughed and told us to tell those cowboys that as they flew by at 75 miles per hour. Maybe then one of them would stop and give you a ride. He laughed and drove away. There, for a while, I thought the guy liked us. I guess not.

He was right. Two different pick-ups drove by and threw beer bottles at us. A crapload of cars cussed us as they passed us. The trucker was right. I had a roll of gauze tape in my duffel bag. I taped "Death in Family" on the side of John's suitcase. Maybe an hour later, a black traveling salesman stopped, picked us up, and gave us a ride into Arlington. He kept asking which one of us had lost a family member. I don't remember who answered. Probably me. John was asleep five minutes after we got in.

Our luck didn't get any better in Arlington. No beer bottles, but we heard every insult you can imagine before John gave up and walked over to the switchman working the tracks running along the highway.

Knowing that John helped restore the old C&S #71 steam engine in Central City might be helpful. I have no idea whether he helped lay track or helped restore the locomotive.

John wasn't known as a truth-teller in those days. He was friendly but tended to make a lot of stuff up. I guessed that when we applied for work in the Schwartzwalder Mine. Why did he get hired as a mucker like me if he was a miner? That would have been an insult to a real miner. Miners were hard to find and made twice the money that muckers made.

Anyway, John talked the switchman into letting us hop in one of the empty boxcars. At first, we were tickled to death that we could say we "hopped a train." By the way, we did ride it "all the way" to Baton Rouge. But unlike Kris Kristofferson, we didn't have a red bandana or Bobby McGee sitting next to us. And, unfortunately, we got out on the wrong side of Baton Rouge. But I'm getting ahead of my story here. So, let me back up a little.

We got on that train just before it went into the switchyards in Arlington or Dallas. I'm not sure where we ended up. The train started and stopped a dozen times. Each time, it left empty cars in one place and hooked up full cars in another. Then, maybe around O' dark-thirty, it started moving, and we were still on it.

The only thing in our private boxcar was some large, empty, folded refrigerator boxes piled up on the wooden floors. This would be the second day without sleep. So John and I decided that we should try to get some rest.

This next part will be hard to swallow, but I swear it's true. The train was going, I'm guessing, sixty miles per hour. If you have never been in a boxcar doing sixty, you might not be able to picture this. It was akin to sitting in a vibrating wooden chair set on high. I woke up as my legs bounced out the door, and my cardboard bed flew out from under me. I grabbed the handle on the door and held on. John grabbed my arms and helped me back in. I was literally flapping in the wind.

An hour later, the train started slowing down, stopping, and starting over and over, and we decided it was time to get out. Finally, we passed a narrow white enamel sign that said, "Baton Rouge." Now, we had some idea where we were, but to this day, I couldn't tell you where Baton Rouge was. We never did see a town.

The sun was starting to rise when the train finally stopped. We took advantage of the opportunity and got off. I looked over at John and started laughing. John looked at me and laughed. We were covered with soot... black soot from the diesel locomotive pulling our boxcar. Either of us could have passed ourselves off as a vaudevillian actor waiting for our next inappropriate show.

A creek was running alongside the tracks down about one hundred yards away. John and I decided it was time to take our first bath in two or maybe three days. So we stripped down to our nothings and started bathing.

John heard it first. Then I heard it. We could hear laughing. Behind some small trees was a wooden bridge. A car full of girls was parked on the bridge, waving to us. We waved back and sat down in the water until they left.

After that, we caught a few short rides and ended up just outside New Orleans. Oh, I forgot to mention. We didn't bring any money with us on this trip. Ten dollars between us, maybe? John thought that having money would make us targets for robbers or something. I thought it would be cool to say we could travel from Denver to Pensacola without cash. I was probably just as much to blame for that little act of stupidity as John.

We were on our second day without eating. We went to a McDonalds and offered to work for food. They offered us each a cheeseburger, fries, and a drink if we would leave. We accepted their kind offer. (That was after we bathed?)

We walked for a long time, trying to catch our next ride. It was late afternoon when we saw an old Chevy sedan pass us and start slowing down. A lady about our age was driving. She came to a complete stop, maybe five hundred feet from where we were standing, and waved for us to come on.

While running to her car, I could see her locking the doors and rolling up the windows. As I said, it was an old car. I'm guessing, but maybe an early fifties Chevy four-door post sedan. She left the front passenger window down about an inch to talk to us.

By the way, this was the number one crazy ride that I alluded to earlier.

John and I stood next to the open window. She looked us over, and then in a heavy Cajun accent, she asked if we planned to rape her if she gave us a ride? We both said no. We just needed a ride to Pensacola. She thought for a minute and asked us if we had any money. We said no. She thought for a minute more and then said, and I quote. "You can't rape the willing, and you can't kill me until my time comes. Get in."

In the next hour, she told us that her husband was a shrimper and went out for two weeks at a time and that he left that morning. She said it had been a long time since she had been in Pensacola, but she needed to stop and get some money first. She turned north on a highway I had never heard of and drove out into the darkest woods we had ever seen. When we finally stopped, we were in front of what might have been an old cotton mill or a bar. I'm not sure which. She told us to wait in the car while she went in to "get" some money.

We waited for about an hour, got scared, and started walking. Neither one of us had any idea where we were. I wasn't even sure what state we were in. Finally, after about thirty minutes, an old man stopped and gave us a ride. He had to be in his eighties. He was driving twenty or twenty-five miles per hour. When we asked him where we were, he told us we were outside Poplarville.

(It gets stranger the further this story goes.)

A few minutes later, red lights flashed behind us, and the local Sheriff pulled the old man over. The old man's name was Mr. Taylor. I know that because that's what the Sheriff called him when the old man rolled down his window. The Sheriff admonished the old man by telling him he should have known better at his age. He asked us to step out of the car and get into the back seat of his cruiser. We complied. He took special care to be sure we put our bags in first.

He informed us that we were under arrest and would spend the night in his jail before seeing the justice of the peace. That changed when he found out that we didn't have any money. That and I told him why we had beards. That seemed to be his primary concern.

He made us empty our bags, and he went through them before letting us repack them. But he kept us in jail. The next morning, he told us we could leave. We made it to the highway before he picked us up again, arrested us for the second time, or whatever he was doing. We weren't sure. This time, he did a complete body search: rubber gloves and all. After not finding anything the second time, he turned us loose again.

John and I walked out of the Sheriff's office and saw a black guy driving a pulpwood log truck. I offered him my watch if he would give us a ride outside of town. His answer told us everything we needed to know. "Naw, sir, I lives here. I can't do that." So we left the highway and started walking into the woods.

I'm not sure how long it took, but we found another highway and started trying to catch a ride again. Finally, a truckload of guys picked us up. They were on their way to work at the Pascagoula Shipyards. They looked scruffier than we did. They dropped us off in Wiggins, Mississippi. The home of the Dizzy Dean Museum.

They let us out just as we were going into town. We saw a policeman up ahead of us. He was directing traffic at a school crossing. When he started walking our way, we started emptying our bags. He laughed and said, "I see you boys have been in Poplarville."

He was the nicest man we met on the whole damned trip. As things like that often turn out, he knew my Dad. My family was from Mississippi. He took us to his office and gifted us a long-distance phone call to Pensacola. I called my Dad and asked him to come and get us. We were maybe an hour and a half from home.

Dad wasn't impressed with my friend, John. He didn't say anything, but I knew. He let us rest for a day and then offered us twenty bucks each to scrape and paint our old house. It was hot, miserable work, and neither John nor I wanted the money that bad. After we finished that day's work, we decided to go to Pensacola Beach for a night out. It was John's first trip to the beach.

Chapter 3: Gelignite

I drank and smoked back then. Neither John nor I had a cigarette or a beer since we left Central City. We needed a break from our break. Our first stop was at a bar near the entrance to the strip. We bought a pack of cigarettes and a beer and sat down with the tourists.

There was this one young lady that caught my eye. She was younger than we were and a whole lot prettier. I noticed that she would stop and talk with people, mostly guys, and then go back outside. A few minutes later, she would repeat the process. I poked John and pointed her out.

She saw us watching her and walked over and started talking to us. And, of course, we bought her a beer. But, as predicted, she left after taking a few sips. Then, five minutes later, she came back empty-handed. So I bought her a second beer, but this time, when she excused herself to go to the restroom, I followed her.

Her boyfriend was sitting in the parking lot, holding the beer that we bought for her. John and I walked over and started a conversation. They were college students down for summer vacation. They planned to get summer jobs to make money for school. They were sleeping in an old cargo van with more dents than I have ever seen in one vehicle.

John told them about Central City and how it went from 400 population one day to 3,500 the next during the summer season. In those days, Central City was an anything-goes summer hangout for tourists. There were twelve bars in Central and another four or five below in Blackhawk. There were also thirteen old closed brothels within those same four blocks. Central

City was primarily a mining town of 3,000 plus population and another 25,000 scattered throughout the surrounding hills during the gold rush. There have been more than 2,200 mining claims filed in Gilpin County. To put everything I just said into perspective, Central City consisted of two blocks of brick buildings coming in and two blocks of brick buildings going out. One giant "T." There were a few buildings scattered outside the city square. Still, most of them were old houses left from the city's hay days when digging for gold was the primary reason to be there.

You might wonder why only brick buildings downtown. At the turn of the century... maybe in 1907?... the Chinese laundry caught fire, and the town went up in flames. All except the assayer's office it was made of brick. The wooden Coeur d'Alene Chapel survived because it was above the city and away from the fire.

Research online if you have doubts about the Chinese laundry starting the fire. There was a strong contingency of Chinese people living and working in Central City and the surrounding area. Look it up.

Because the town was rebuilt in brick, it was still in good repair and usable as a tourist town. Thus, the population boom each year.

When John finished telling the young man and girl about Central City, they both wanted to go back with us and work there for the summer. So, we had our ride back to Colorado. Between the four of us, we might have had thirty dollars. Gas was around 25 cents a gallon back then. Thirty dollars would buy a lot of gas. But, as it turned out, not enough to get to Central City. We did some horse trading at our last fill-up. We didn't need a spare tire nearly as much as we needed gas.

The young lady chickened out in Dallas, and we dropped her off at her aunt's house. The guy went to Central City and found a job at the Teller House waiting tables. He made a little over six thousand dollars in tips that summer, plus a modest salary. Teller House employees lived and ate in the hotel. It was part of their compensation. Six grand after expenses was a lot of money back then.

That was the year that "Harvey" played in the Opera House. Gig Young, Jesse White (The original Maytag repairman and the only one in the original movie.), Dort Clark, and Spring Byington all lived in the Teller House that summer. Denver Charter buses came to Central City in caravans that year.

The usual thousands of young people still showed up. As in the past, they came to the mountains to blow off steam and get drunk. It was a crazy year. Hundreds of folks in evening dresses and suits and thousands of hippies and college students walked around together. All were having a good time. It was a good year if you were working in Central City.

Just in case anyone wants to know, Jesse White was a prick. Within two weeks, he was barred from every bar and restaurant in town. They would bring food to his room, but no one would serve him in their restaurants or bars.

On the other hand, Dort Clark was a great guy. He was down-to-earth and an honest character. He was a character actor. After meeting him, I started looking for him in old movies. He was in half of every western I watched. He loved telling stories about the movies he was in. The stars he worked with. He didn't have a bad word to say about any of them. His stories were funny.

We never saw Gig Young or Spring Byington. I understand Miss Byington died of cancer right after that summer. She was a native of Colorado Springs, Colorado. Gig Young stayed in his room.

I took a job waiting tables in the Toll-Gate Tavern, and later, I managed a bar downstairs called Madam Gales. Madam Gales was a locals-only bar. A place to get away from the tourists and craziness. Her seating capacity was around 50.

The Toll House, the upstairs bar, was in a huge building that held maybe five hundred people on the main floor and perhaps another hundred on the balconies. That's a guess on my part. I never counted.

When and if he worked, my buddy John Johnson worked for his Dad at Johnson's Smorgasbord or the Gold Coin.

One more story about Central City that's too good to let go untold.

I had a lot of experience using "mine-gel" while I worked in the mine. Some of the rocks we were there to break up were too large to do efficiently with a double-jack. A few were as large as a Volkswagen Bug; others were close to that size. We blasted them and then finished breaking them with our sledgehammers.

I think the real name for mine-gel was gelignite. This story is about a stick of mine-gel that a friend brought home in his lunch pail.

I shouldn't use his name, so I'll call him "Fred." I doubt that he's still around, but just in case, Fred, it'll be.

Fred had a stick of mine gel and wanted to get rid of it. He was afraid one of his buddies would take it and do something stupid, and it would come back on him. So I told Fred I had a good use for it and told him my plan.

I was staying in the Chain of Mines Hotel at the time. My room looked down on Lawrence Street. Lawrence was the one-way street coming into Central City. Gregory was the street going back down to Black Hawk. They joined again down below between the two cities. In the gap between the two roads, a large ravine with two flumes ran under Central City and opened down below where the creek came out again.

I think the townspeople added the two flumes to the original creek bed, covered the ravine, and built Central City above the creek. Free land.

These flumes were large. I remember standing and reaching out and up, trying to touch the opposite sides and not being able to do so. These two flumes ran side by side, carried the creek under and beyond Central City, and emptied back into the original bed. Finally, it emptied down below in Black Hawk and into the much larger Clear Creek.

Those flumes also carried most of the liquid waste from Central City. With that in mind, we had one urinal in Madam Gales designated for Coors drinkers only. We served Coors, Michelob, and Bud. We told them that we were part of the recycling center for Coors Brewery down in Golden. Clear Creek ran through Golden and Coors. Telling you all this will help you understand the rest of this story.

Fred and I went down between Gregory and Lawrence, where the two flumes emptied back into the ravine and placed a large flat rock in the stream just at the openings of those flumes. I set that rock maybe a quarter of an inch above the waterline. This part is important.

I used to enjoy standing at the head of those flumes and singing. I could hear my voice echoing up those flumes and under the city.

I smoothed out the gel on top of that rock and added a ten-minute fuse. Then, Fred and I walked casually back to our rooms. He was staying in the "Ramstader Arms," and I was in the Chain of Mines Hotel. Our rooms were across from each other and close enough that we could talk in a normal voice and hear each other across the street.

After some thought, I ran downstairs to the lobby. I got change from the clerk for the cigarette machine, bought a pack, and then went back up and waited. I had my alibi.

Fred started getting excited and pointing behind the hotel. I couldn't see what he was pointing at until the Sheriff passed the mine gel. It went off when the Sheriff was maybe fifty feet past. The ravine was fifteen feet deep where we set the charge, so I doubt the Sheriff saw anything, but he sure felt and heard it.

So did everyone else in town. Within minutes, the streets looked like a Gene Wilder and Mel Brooks movie. Young Frankenstein comes to mind first. People with shotguns, rifles, shovels, and God knows what else was running through the streets. The whole town was there.

If anyone else knew that it was us, no one told. There was no damage to anything other than a few people's nerves. Laying the gel on the flat rock caused the force of the blast to go up. There wasn't even a mark on the rock. If I had laid a sheet of paper on top, it would have blown a hole large enough to bury a school bus... but I didn't.

That was the center of all conversations for at least a week. One fellow liked talking about it a lot. His name was Willy. Willy worked down in Black Hawk at the newspaper. Our little caper made the headlines. The circulation was maybe 500.

A week later, someone dropped what was estimated as several sticks of mine gel down the manhole cover on Main Street. It blew out all the windows on the street and damaged some of the storefronts. The manhole cover went straight up, then came back down through the roof of the Smorgasbord, on down through the third floor, second floor, first floor, and buried itself in the sod basement floor. It was deep enough that they debated digging it up. I don't know if they ever did. By they, I mean the F.B.I. They were treating this one as a domestic terrorist attack. This was before that was a thing.

We all knew who did it, but we didn't want Willy going to jail or, in his case, probably a mental institution. Unfortunately, Willy was a little short on common sense and IQ. This time, it was the center of conversations for almost a month.

Willy thought that it was funny. So he decided to do it again. So the next time, he wrapped a pine tree with sticks of mine gel, taped it together with duct tape, and then set it off above Black Hawk. More specifically, above the newspaper editor's home, maybe a hundred feet below.

Half the side of the hill came down with all the boulders within. The editor's house was gone. Only two walls were left standing. These were the two between the slope and the editor's bed. One neat "V" shaped section of his house kept him from being buried alive.

This time, they came and picked up Willy, and I don't know where they took him. We didn't see or hear of Willy again that year. (True Story, I swear.)

Chapter 4: Growing Up

It's always a good idea to read what you write. After reading my first two chapters, you might think I sounded crazy. Maybe I should give you some background on my mental state at the time. So, I'll start from the beginning. This will be the Reader's Digest version.

While I was growing up, my Dad was a fireman at Pensacola Naval Air Station, and he owned a fire extinguisher business. I helped him with the business as soon as I was old enough to ride along.

Helping Dad meant I was required to lift heavy CO_2 tanks daily. The fifty-pounders weighed one-hundred-plus pounds when filled with CO_2. My body was well developed. I finished growing up at age fourteen. I don't know if those two things were related, but I grew up fast physically. For me, going through adolescence was no big deal. I looked like a grownup; therefore, I was treated like one. It seemed reasonable for me to act like a grownup.

Dad worked long hours at the fire station. Twenty-four on and twenty-four off. On his day off, he worked his fire extinguisher business. It was a thriving business and kept him busy most of his "time off." That left mother to fend for herself most of the time. On my fourteenth birthday, my mother took me to the DMV to get my learner's permit. I drove the car there and back home. I had to. Mother couldn't drive. She never learned. I started driving my mother to the grocery store and church when I was fourteen.

When I started high school, my size was an advantage. The High School I attended was new. Seniors, Juniors, Sophomores, and Freshmen were all new to the school. Yes, it was a four-year high school. So, because I looked like a Senior, I was treated like one. Seniors could haze freshmen. No one bothered me. I was muscular and athletic in appearance, so I was never challenged. But, because I looked and was treated like a Senior, I acted like one. Or at least more than the other kids my age did. It seemed reasonable to me.

Please don't misunderstand; I may have looked like a senior, but I was a freshman. I was expected to act as a senior, but the truth was, I didn't have any idea how that was. I lacked the most essential thing that a senior would have had... experience.

I was raised in the Mormon faith. That didn't help, either. I was treated the same at church. If this sounds like me whining, I apologize. I'm not complaining or making excuses for my future behavior. I'm old enough now that I understand more about whining. To affect an outcome, whining must happen before or during, not after.

Anyway, I was given responsibilities I had no idea how to handle. So, I did what I thought I was supposed to do. When I graduated from High School, I got married. I had no job skills, so I joined the military. My parents encouraged me to join. My mother even rode with me to the recruiter. In retrospect, it may have been the smartest thing I could have done. Maybe. The jury is still out on that one.

My father was in the Army Air Force during World War II. Back then, the Air Force was a branch of the Army. He was a bombardier instructor. That's why I elected to join the Army, not the Navy, even though I lived in Pensacola. Dad worked at Pensacola, N.A.S., and I still wanted to join the Army.

Because of my test scores, I was placed in the Army Security Agency. A.S.A. was an intelligence-gathering branch. I spent a year at Fort Devens, Massachusetts, and two years at Itazuki Air Force Base, Hakata Annex, Japan.

Yes, I was still in the Army. In the Military Intelligence community, combined service bases were not uncommon.

When it was time to get out, I offered to re-enlist if they would let me go to Officer Candidate School. O.C.S. The best they would offer was a chance to be interviewed, but I still agreed. Somewhere in the back of my head, I knew I would make it. I always believed that I was leading a charmed life.

I should stop here. That wasn't true. I promised that I wouldn't lie writing this book. What I am about to admit will make me sound arrogant. I'm not, or I try not to be, whichever. I believed that I was put here on earth with a purpose. I didn't think that my life was preordained. But I did feel that I was preordained to do something special. I didn't know then, and I don't know now what I was sent here for. But so that you know, I still believe I was... I am here for a reason. Honestly, I always thought it had something to do with my children. I'm not sure why I felt that way. It was something inside. It wasn't anything I could ever put into words.

This will disappoint my family. I never believed it had anything to do with the Mormon Church. I was raised Mormon. I followed the Mormon teachings. I gave my best effort, but deep down inside, I knew I wasn't cut out to be what I was pretending to be. It wasn't a conscious decision so much as a realization.

Anyway, back to my story.

 When it was time for me to re-enlist, I had two children and a wife, and I still didn't have a trade that would translate from military life to civilian life. But I still believed that things always worked out for the best. Luck was on my side, I think. I was accepted into O.C.S. My test scores were high enough, but the Oral Board interview got me in.

But I found a way to screw it up. Two weeks before I graduated from O.C.S., I was offered a chance to attend flight school. I accepted. In a year, I went from a non-combatant in the Army Security Agency to a possible combatant in the Signal Corps. But the minute I raised my hand that day, I went into training to become an avenging angel in service to the Gods of War. That's how I felt about helicopter pilots in Vietnam. Now, I would be one of the special ones trained to reign down fury from the heavens. I would be a helicopter pilot.

I wrote what follows many years ago. It seems appropriate here. "Each year, we send offerings to the "Gods of War." We send only the best and bravest among us in hopes that the Gods will be satisfied with our offerings. We do this so that we can continue to live in the greatest nation ever to inhabit this earth."

But the question is, why do we continue to feed these Gods of War after we have achieved the peace we were seeking? Were we afraid that peace would end if we stopped? So we keep sending our offerings. We know that the cost of peace is ongoing. It will never end so long as we have something so valuable in our possession. There will always be someone in the world who will want to take it from us. Not for themselves. They know that if others see what we have, they will want it, too. So, we continue to send our youth to do what our old cannot.

I read somewhere once that the best way to achieve world peace was to send our ambassadors to fight our wars. I like that idea.

Chapter 5: O.C.S.

I arrived at Fort Gordon's Signal Corp Officer Candidate School, weighing 235 pounds. Four weeks later, I weighed forty pounds less. Not possible, you say. I'm here to tell you that it was possible and that I did it. I probably wouldn't have lost forty pounds if it were diet alone. But diet was just the first half. The extreme exercise was the other. Together, they were the perfect combination.

Our meals lasted three minutes. No bite could be larger than "thumbnail size." We ate "square meals." You scooped up four or five pieces of corn on your fork and lifted them straight to nose level. Then, in one smooth motion, you guided your fork back to your mouth. You were allowed three chews, and then you were expected to swallow. While chewing, you followed the same process in reverse. After laying your fork beside your plate, you returned your hand to the tabletop. You were ready to repeat the process and take your second bite... unless someone asked for salt. God forbid that anyone asked for salt.

We were Basic Candidates. Asking for salt or any condiment on the table was a five-act play. First, you asked if any Tact Officer at your table wanted salt. If one did, you passed the salt to that officer. When he finished, you asked if any Senior at your table wanted salt. You repeated the process. Then you checked with the Junior Candidates. Finally, you asked your fellow candidates if they wanted salt. By then, your three minutes were up, and step five never happened.

It was time to get your ass chewed out for taking food you didn't eat. This often led to multiple push-ups as punishment. However, you soon learned to enjoy unseasoned food.

As far as the exercise portion of this diet was concerned, listen to the following. When we arrived at O.C.S., we didn't know what was expected of us. No one told us what we could or couldn't do. We learned by the push-up method. For example, we were issued new, heavily starched fatigues. We often changed fatigues twice a day. Sometimes more. When fatigues were new, they usually had loose threads on the seams. If your tact officer saw one of these, he pulled it, and you were expected to recoil and go, "Boom." Much like a cannon. The loose threads were referred to as lanyards. If your Boom wasn't loud enough, or you took too long to go boom, your Tact Officer would tell you to drop and give him "ten." That was ten perfect push-ups. No one ever did a perfect push-up. So, your Tact Officer would stop you and tell you to start over. He did this until you got it right. Usually, the Tact Officer got bored and walked away before your arms gave out and you couldn't do another push-up. If you cheated and stood up because he walked away, you were in more trouble than before. He would drop you again and ask why you got up before you finished. This usually meant three or four minutes of holding yourself up and trying not to give out while he was watching.

Tact Officers loved teaming up on basic candidates. You learned to look for the second officer before you stood up. We soon knew that if you couldn't see him, he was standing directly behind you. My Tact Officer's favorite name for me was "screw-head."

We weren't allowed to walk anywhere as Basic Candidates. When two of us were going in the same direction, we formed a formation and ran in step. Two or fifty, when we ran, we stayed in step.

Lights out were at twenty-two hundred hours (10 pm), but you always had more work than time, so you finished what needed to be done in the dark while someone watched for the barracks guard. We were all required to pull jobs that kept us up while others slept. Latrine duty, fireman (We had coal furnaces), and guard duty all required staying up at night. That was lost sleep. You didn't get naps to make up for lost sleep.

Looking anywhere other than straight ahead was an offense. Whispering to the candidate next to you was an offense... even if you told him to shut up. If you committed an offense, everyone paid. If he committed an offense, you paid. You were a team. If one man faltered, we were all punished. The greater the offense, the higher the number of push-ups.

Speaking of push-ups. We were expected to do ten perfect push-ups for the first three weeks. The first week we were there was referred to as zero week. O.C.S. lasted twenty-three weeks. Starting week two, three the real way people counted, we added five push-ups to what was expected. 10, 15, 20, 25, 30, 35, 40, 45, and we stopped and held at 50. That didn't matter. By that time, we could do push-ups in our sleep.

So that there are no misunderstandings, we did things other than eating and push-ups. Usually, the first half of the day was spent in classrooms and the second half in the field. They loved taking us on nature walks. Ten, fifteen, and even twenty-mile hikes were not uncommon. Sometimes, we marched. Other times, we ran with full packs and rifles.

Funny story. They loved coming into the barracks and inspecting our areas. If one man failed because a toothbrush was not straight or there was a wrinkle in one of his folded towels, we were all punished with special forms of punishment. My personal favorite was the "Dying Cockroach." The dying cockroach was a punishment where you laid on your back and held your arms, legs, and head upright. If someone, anyone, let their head touch the floor, everyone started over. I was famous for falling asleep in that position once. Honest.

I should explain. These barracks were World War II-style wooden buildings. Inside walls were two-by-fours, and whatever lumber was used for the outside wall. No insulation. The floors were those wide strips of green linoleum with thousands of coats of wax on them. Everything else was painted white. There were open places between the walls and the roof that you could have thrown a cat through. That helped during the summer. It sucked when it got cold... that and the sulfur smell that came with the coal.

We were learning how to work under stress as a single unit, and they watched how we reacted when we were under extreme pressure and very tired. A Tact Officer's favorite thing to do was ask if you wanted to quit. They made it sound so good. "No one will think any less of you if you do." They were wrong. I would have.

We were learning how to work together. That was important, but the most important lesson we learned was that we all had weaknesses alone. Together, we were unbeatable.

I remember one twenty-mile run with full packs and rifles. We were well past the halfway point in our training and in good shape. But one man was older than the rest of us. I don't remember exactly how old he was. He might have been thirty or thirty-one years old. Too old to be doing what we were doing. His body took longer to recover between runs. I think his body took longer to get into the shape the rest of us were already in.

After eighteen miles, he was all in. He fell. A couple of us ran back, picked him up, and helped him keep going. When we were tired, other candidates dropped back and relieved us. This went on until we were carrying him. He never gave up on us, and we never let him give up on himself. We all made it back to camp together. That night, the Tact Officers walked into the barracks at nine and turned out the lights. The next day was Sunday, and we knew there wouldn't be any inspections. Sundays were our free days. We could rest until noon. Lord, help us Sunday afternoon.

There was this one candidate that made it into O.C.S. that I never understood how he passed the physicals. His name was Kline. Kline was a genius. He often corrected our instructors during classes... in a good way. He would engage them in conversations that caused them to stop what they were doing and take notes. He wasn't arrogant. He knew everything, but he couldn't tie his bootlaces. Now that I think about it, the Tact Officers never screwed with the guy. They knew something about the guy that we didn't.

We tried helping him whenever we could. We polished his brass and his boots. While we were doing that, he would help anyone who needed help with that day's lessons. We even made sure his gig line was straight before inspections. These were things that he couldn't understand. He was as baffled about lining up gig lines as we were about why we had to study something unrelated to becoming an officer. He was a great guy, but he would never be a squad leader in combat. We all knew that, and we hoped the Army did.

Near the end of our O.C.S. training, we had a visitor. He was considered important enough that we were pulled out of training and held a formation to listen to what he had to say. He didn't waste any words. "If anyone here would like to go to flight school, see me after this meeting.

You have your Tact Officer's permission." There wasn't any long-winded explanation, no promises. That was all he said.

I was the first one in line. Now that I think of it, I might have been the only one in that line. I couldn't wait. Long before I re-enlisted, I discovered that my father was trying to arrange an interview for me to apply for Annapolis. I was told that Congressman Bob Sikes was involved. My father was so disappointed in me for eloping right out of high school and screwing it up that he never talked to me about it directly. His dream for me was that I would be able to do what he never had a chance to do while he was in the military. He wanted me to become an officer and a pilot. I saw this as my chance to redeem myself with my father, and I took it. Besides, what better way can you think of for me to overcome my fear of heights?

The one obstacle that I didn't foresee was a little more personal. One of the conditions for getting into flight school was passing the physical. I was in the best condition of my life. By now, I was down to 179 pounds. I was so trim that my mother cried when she came to my graduation ceremony. She kept asking me if she could go and get me something to eat.

I could run for hours without resting. I could do 75 push-ups without breaking a sweat. I felt better than at any time before or since. Not passing my physical never entered my mind.

Thank God they needed Pilots in Vietnam. Everything went great until the medic checked my blood pressure. It was too high. The medic asked me if I was "anxious" about passing the physical. I told him that I wasn't. He tried again, and still, it was elevated. He asked me to wait thirty minutes and said he would try again. It was still too high.

That's when he told me that pilots weren't allowed to take blood pressure medications and fly, and it looked like I needed them. I don't remember what I said to change his mind, but I remember convincing him to give it one more try. He asked me if I minded taking a nap before he tried again. I didn't mind. I woke up as he was pulling off the blood pressure cuff and saw him smiling. "You passed."

Back to my story about Candidate Kline.

Graduation day came, and they told us he wouldn't attend the ceremony. They told us not to worry about Kline, he would graduate with the next class. His security clearance hadn't been completed. He came from Greenwich Village, New York. There were rumors that it might have had something to do with his parents. I never heard the whole story. His name was on the list of candidates that graduated. I heard later that his orders came two months later, and he was sent to Washington, DC. He would have been the twenty-seventh man to graduate from our class. We started with fifty-two candidates and graduated twenty-six. We were one of the better classes. 50%

of our class graduated. We were class number 17. Signal Corp O.C.S. was new.

Most of our graduation ceremony was uneventful, except for the newly commissioned 2nd Lt. Adams' portion. Adams gave the opening introductions.

He started by acknowledging Major General Walter B. Richardson and his wife, Mrs. Richardson. Then he introduced the Signal Training Center Commandant, Colonel Raymond H. Bates, his wife, Mrs. Bates, and their son, Master Bates. I swear that's the truth... "and their son, Master Bates." The Colonel's kid was twelve or thirteen years old.

No one said a word. Lieutenant Adams had followed the manual to the letter. We all knew he planned to do it, but none of us believed he would say those words. Adams was a Special Forces sergeant before he applied for O.C.S. The guy had nuts as big as coconuts.

Side note: I've often had enlisted men come to me and ask if I thought O.C.S. was worth the effort. I always told them how it helped me become a better man. I told them how great it was to be an officer. Of course, it was better, but I never had it all that bad while enlisted. So, I lied to them. If I had been honest, I would have told them that no one in their right mind would ever apply for O.C.S. if they knew what they were getting into. Don't tell anyone that I said that.

Chapter 6: Primary Flight School

For clarification purposes, I need to explain. Army helicopter pilots went to two different flight schools at two different locations. Primary Flight Training took place at Fort Wolters, Texas. Fort Wolters was just outside of Mineral Wells. Draw a straight line across a sheet of paper from side to side. At the Eastern end, put Dallas, then Arlington, then Fort Worth, Weatherford, and on the western end, finish with Mineral Wells and Ft. Wolters. Make sure that Ft. Worth is about in the middle. That's how I was told to picture where Ft. Wolters was located when I asked where in hell Mineral Wells was.

They could have told me that it was in the middle of the closest thing to a desert you could find in Texas, but I think they were trying to be nice. It's a pleasant place to live with lots of friendly people, especially if you enjoy warm weather.

I drove a fairly new 1966 Ford Galaxie 500 convertible. Dark green with a black top, dark green vinyl seats... and no air. It cost me $2300 new. I remember the salesman laughing when I asked why it didn't have an air conditioner. "It's a convertible, son. How much air do you need? Sign here." I signed the paper and drove home with the top down. It was fall and beautiful. I remember thinking how silly I must have sounded, asking my salesman why a convertible didn't have air.

A month after I arrived at Fort Wolters, I would have given a hundred dollars for five minutes with that guy in a dark alley.

I was full of good decisions in those days. I rented a small trailer without air conditioning for my wife and me. As I said, a month later, it got hot. That part of Texas was that way. It was nice one day, hot the next day, and almost every day after that for seven or eight months.

Long story made short. The Hiller OH-23 Raven helicopters we trained in didn't have air conditioners either. You sat in a fiberglass bubble wearing a long-sleeved flight suit, gloves, boots, and a helmet. I took my basic flying lessons in the Hiller Raven. It was suitable for what it was used for. It was reliable and stable and could take a lot of abuse. The Warrant Officer Candidates flew the Hughes TH-55 Osage helicopters. I wasn't impressed. They liked them, but I didn't trust anything with six fan belts holding me in the air. On the other side of the field, we call them Mattel Messerschmitts.

My flight instructor at Ft. Wolters was named Toth. Mr. Toth was Hungarian and had a strong Hungarian accent. English was almost a second language for him. He worked for Southern Airways. Southern Airways had contracts with the Army and provided virtually all our instructors. I found it curious that the Army used civilians to train their pilots, not their own pilots.

Mr. Toth had been a helicopter pilot in the Army. When he got out of the Army, he went to work for Southern Airways as a student instructor.

His story was that his family fled Europe when the communists started taking over Hungary. Later, when he tried to join our Army, they discovered that he had been a soccer star in Hungary. So, he was first sent to basic training and then assigned to the Special Services soccer team to serve the remainder of his enlistment.

Mr. Toth told me that he was treated like a king until he broke his ankle and couldn't play soccer. He said the Army wasn't sure what to do with him after that. Finally, their solution was to send him to flight school and make him a Warrant Officer and Pilot. He served the rest of his time and pulled one tour in Vietnam before he got out.

Besides being difficult to understand, especially when he got excited and reverted to his mother tongue, Mr. Toth was an excellent instructor. He was given all the problematic students. I was assigned to him during my second day of actual flight training. After that, we had several days of ground training before we climbed into our first cockpit. It wasn't because I was a lousy student. Remember why I asked for flight training? My fear of heights.

It took me a few hours longer to hover than most other officers. But my turning point was when Mr. Toth took me out on our first flight away from the airfield. I was flying the chopper. Mr. Toth asked me if I had control, and I answered that I did. I saw Mr. Toth lower the visor on his helmet, remove his hands from the controls, and put his feet on the console. That scared me. He always held the controls in the past in case I made a mistake. He could recover control of the aircraft quicker if he were already holding the controls.

There was a long silence before he spoke again. Then, calmly, he asked me if everything was alright. His soft voice, without his usual accent, scared me. I knew that I was doing something wrong. I looked at all my instruments. Horizon was good. Engine and blade rpm were right on. Everything looked golden. I answered yes. A few minutes later, he asked me again. Before I answered, he said, "Look outside."

I almost shit my pants. I was down in the trees. I looked off to my side and saw what should have been below. We were in the trees, not at the thousand-foot level I was supposed to be flying at. It scared me so bad that I pulled in power and climbed back up where I was supposed to be. That was the day that my fear of heights climbed a thousand feet. It was where I felt safe. Flying between tree-tops and a thousand feet became my comfort zone. Later, in Vietnam, I learned that the safest places to be were either tree-top or at three thousand feet or higher.

I was the first one in my class to solo. I had ten hours and thirty minutes of stick time.

We flew hours and hours of flight patterns at our stage fields. Each stage field had a tower and at least one short runway designed for choppers, not fixed-winged aircraft, to land at one end, hover down to the other, and take off again. This was as much for teaching us how to work with the air traffic controllers as for taking off and landing during flight patterns.

One day, Mr. Toth stepped out of the aircraft and told me to take it back to the base. That was the day I got to be one of the links in the "Daisy Chain." If you can imagine hundreds of helicopters lined up nose to asshole as far as the eye could see, that's what it was like flying back solo for the first time. For some, like me, it was my first time in the chain. Others were probably pros. But the majority were someplace in between and still learning to deal with all the starts and stops.

I'm not sure I can describe it adequately, but imagine holding a rope and whipping it up, then down, and watching the curls run down the length of the rope. That's what it looked like from the rear. I was waiting for someone to do something stupid and kill us all. Just being there scared the crap out of me.

Toth was fun to ride with. He had the air of an experienced combat Pilot about him. He was flexible. He didn't panic. One day, we would fly over the flatlands, and he would take the controls and fly down low enough to see inside barns and old sheds. He admitted to me later that he was looking for old cars. He loved antique cars.

Other times, we would fly between the high banks of a winding riverbed, learning to judge turns and working on reaction time. I don't think that was in the training manual, but it was fun, and I learned a lot from it. I felt like I was a better Pilot because of it.

Other times, we would climb to three thousand feet and fly from one point to another, watching the ground for places to land if the engine failed. Then, Toth would wait for me to get comfortable and start daydreaming... or get preoccupied looking for old cars. Then, he would cut power and let me practice autorotations.

I loved autorotations. The blades on a helicopter were its wings. If you keep your blades turning, you can still fly, even without power. When the wind passes through your blades, they're spinning. Much like the pinwheels you played with as a kid. The more wind, the faster they turn.

Like blowing at a pinwheel, falling caused your blades to turn, and they continued acting as wings. However, handled properly, you could make a smoother landing autorotating than with power.

First, nose up slightly and dump pitch. (Flatten your blades) Next, if you haven't already, start looking for a clearing to sit down in. Then, circle until you have that spot in sight. Always watch your blade R.P.M. If you bleed off too much R.P.M., you'll start falling. At seventy-five feet above the ground, start pulling in pitch and nosing up. Start slowing down. Too far above seventy-five feet, you will run out of lift before you touch down and have a hard landing. But if you do it right, you can flare around fifteen feet and start pulling in pitch again, and you'll settle down to earth as smooth as silk. I remember Toth telling me, "Trust me, knowing how to do this will come in handy if you get shot down later." He was right.

Note: It's been more than fifty years since I performed an autorotation. Every aircraft has a place where it's happiest during an autorotation. So please don't send me letters telling me how you do them. I don't fly anymore, so I don't care.

Toth had a Turk, a couple of Swedes, a Vietnamese, and lots of guys like me as students. It's the Turk that this story is about.

Toth had a Turkish Officer who wouldn't apply himself. He spent too much time in the officer's club. Before hearing the end of this story, you might have believed that he was incompetent or couldn't learn how to fly. He had an Uncle that pulled strings and got him promoted in the Turkish military. (I've heard stories about Turks in the military during World War II. Everyone feared them. They were good.)

This guy wasn't one of those guys. He was in his twenty-second week and still hadn't flown solo. The story goes that they decided to wash him out of the program and send him home. So we (the U.S.) sent a message asking the Turks to return him to Turkey. Within minutes, we received a message telling us to "Shoot him there and save us the airfare." Several personal calls later, we found out that they were serious.

Toth and the Turk took one chopper, and another Pilot flew a second chopper out as far as they could from the base and landed. Toth explained to the Turk what they were doing. "We aren't going to shoot you. You'll have to kill yourself. Either fly this chopper back or crash and kill yourself trying. Or you can sit out here, starve to death, and let the coyotes eat you. We don't care which."

That was the day that the Turk learned to fly solo. He turned out to be a good Pilot once he applied himself.

That's the kind of guy that Toth was.

Chapter 7: Advanced Flight School

The second half of my training, Advanced Flight School, took place at Fort Rucker, Alabama, just outside of Enterprise. That's not right.

Fort Rucker sits on sixty-two thousand acres. It's pretty much the center of activity for that area. Enterprise is famous for a boll weevil statue in the middle of a roundabout. Rucker is renowned for producing great Pilots. Saying that Rucker sits next to Enterprise would be like saying that the mountain sits next to Mohamad. I remember living there with my wife and two children and how unfriendly the people were to the military.

I like to keep things in proper focus. I could write a new chapter here if I wanted to waste my time. There were lots of towns where the locals were unfriendly. Enterprise just happened to be the worst of them. Talking about people who lived near a military base and how little they appreciated the money that the military brought to their city would be a waste of time. That was fifty-plus years ago. Surely, they have learned something by now.

Fort Rucker gave me two things that I didn't get in Wolters. First, I learned to fly by instruments; second, I learned to fly the Cadillac of helicopters, the Huey UH-1.

Hueys were sweet. It's impossible for me to adequately explain why the Army gave the Bell Iroquois helicopter such an uncomplimentary nickname as the "Huey." I loved them more than any other aircraft I flew. Saying that Huey was the Cadillac of choppers doesn't do Huey justice. The Huey was a cross between a Cadillac and a Peterbilt or a Lincoln and a Freightliner if you are so inclined. I remember one guy saying that the Huey was akin to a Checker Cab on steroids. He probably flew slicks. You pick. I don't care. In my mind, the Huey was the most versatile aircraft ever built. It was the best medivac, troop hauler, freight hauling, gunship flying, observation platform, and most versatile aircraft ever used in battle. But that's just my opinion.

Flying at Ft. Rucker was more formal than Wolters. We knew how to fly. Now, we were being taught the skills that we would need in Vietnam. Long cross-country flights were frequent. We participated in "escape and evasion" games with the Rangers. But learning to fly with cargo or practicing cross country seemed to be their focus.

Not every pilot did well in the cross-country flights. One pilot seemed to get lost during every one of our three-legged cross countries. However, only one of these cross-country flights is worth remembering. This flight was the last and longest of all our flights and was a three-legger. One pilot flew, and one navigated. Lt. White was the navigator.

We referred to it as the White incident. During this exercise, everyone involved, except Lt. White, finished their cross-country flight within the allotted time. At this point in our training, we were almost ready for our first duty station. That would be Vietnam in 95% of the cases. We were in the home stretch.

This flight started by heading East from Point A toward point B, then South to point C, and finally, back to point A. Picture a triangle in your mind. We were supposed to call in at each landmark along the way and at each corner of our triangle. Water towers, railroad tracks, barns with markings, silos, and remote staging fields that we had flown to before. All of these were marked on our maps and, if followed, would guide us to point A, point B, and finally back to the beginning, point C.

Our job was to adjust for crosswinds and to follow the markers given to us. We had already learned how to crab. Crabbing was aiming the nose of the chopper in one direction but being pushed by the wind in another direction.

Our instructors warned us about getting lost. They told us that getting lost wasn't the greatest sin. Getting lost and not admitting it was.

Lt. White's team called in at Point A but did not call the tower after that. Finally, worried that he might have crashed, the tower started trying to raise White's team on the radio. When White finally responded and reported that he was lost, the tower asked Lt. White to give them any visual landmarks around his chopper.

After several questions, White said he could see a large lake up ahead. The tower asked how large. White's answer told them what they needed to know. He said that it was the largest lake he had ever seen.

Right then, another voice came across the airways and said he had an Army helicopter in sight and would verify the tail number. It was White. The big lake that he could see was the Gulf of Mexico. White was presently flying over a restricted area on Eglin Air Force Base. He now had two Air Force jets circling him, and one of them offered to either shoot him down or escort him back to his base. His choice.

Despite White's shortcomings as a navigator, he was a good Pilot. I figure the Army knew there would be another Pilot and two crewmen in his helicopter when he flew in Nam. At least one could show White how to get wherever he was going. Nothing was ever repeated about that incident.

Chapter 8: The Long Flight

After graduating from flight school, half of our class left for Vietnam the following week. They had a few days to arrange their affairs and say goodbye to loved ones. My orders gave me three weeks. I was able to spend Christmas with my family before I left.

I boarded my flight to Vietnam, along with as many others as the aircraft would hold. Most were enlisted men making their first trip overseas. We stopped in Alaska and were allowed to get out of the aircraft and walk around. I don't remember there being a terminal. If there was, it wasn't close, and it was dark. We walked around on the tarmac while they refueled. I don't know where we were in Alaska, except that it was frozen solid and cold. I don't think that they were worried about anyone running away.

Our next stop was Tan Son Nhut Air Force Base, somewhere outside Saigon. Tan Son Nhut was a Vietnamese Military base used by the U.S. as a major base during the war. We arrived in early January, maybe the second or third of January 1968. The great Tet Offensive was starting, but not officially.

The airfield was lit up like Broadway on New Year's Eve. We could hear mortars coming in and hurried off the Plane and onto what looked like a white school bus filled with sandbags up to the windows. We were told not to worry about our luggage. It would follow. It didn't. They had us sit on the bus floor while they drove across the field to the "terminal."

Between the long lines and hours of waiting at the beginning of that flight and my stay at Tan Son Nhut, I had no idea what day it was. Time had already lost any meaning.

We were greeted and sorted several times in the next few days. The khakis I was wearing were starting to get ripe. But I still smelled better than my hosts. So far, enlisted men and officers were being held together. We were all being treated equally, at least in the beginning. The next day, I was put on a C-130 cargo plane and flown to Qui Nhon. After that, I was flown by helicopter to my new base, Lane A.H.P., in An Son.

Later, people asked me if it was scary for the first few days. Sure, I guess. But, in truth, it was too surreal to be scary. It was more like being in a daze. Mostly, I was happy that I kept ending up in the right places. Not once did anyone ask me where I was going or how I was getting there. There were even new clothes and quarters waiting for me when I arrived. Ranks and insignias were even sown on. Then, it was time for me to take my first bath since I left the U.S. I was no longer the best-smelling guy in the room.

I was assigned to the 61st Assault Helicopter Company. I didn't know it then, but my unit had only been declared operational on December 20, 1967. I arrived three weeks later. The original concept of an A.H.C. was already changing and evolving. New units were coming to Vietnam with that designation. How they were being used was changing. Assault Helicopter Companies in Vietnam were being remodeled day to day based on what they were learning. I thought that the confusion was because my unit was new. It was, but so were all the other Assault Helicopter Companies. Some were not as new as the 61st A.H.C., but how they were deployed changed daily.

I was new and learning how to work in a combat zone. My unit had only been in the country three weeks longer than I had. It was a mess; even someone as new as me could see it.

Mostly, we were flying milk runs—hauling supplies or troops from one point to another. Occasionally, we flew officers out into the field so they could see firsthand what was happening.

But one by one, new missions were being added... actual combat missions. We were flying Special Forces Advisers out to firebases. Those were usually deep into the mountains and jungles. We were beginning to feel like we were something other than taxis. The only good I could see from what we were doing was learning our way around.

When our unit was put together, most came from Ft. Campbell with the unit. But they were adding to and trading people, trying to even out the odds. At least, that's how I thought about what was going on. We were getting experienced door Gunners and Crew Chiefs. Pilots were coming from other units. Even our commander changed a month or two after I arrived.

We were adjusting and learning. We were doing whatever was asked of us. We were flying supplies, picking up the wounded and dead. At first, I didn't understand picking up dead soldiers in the middle of a firefight. We were putting ourselves in danger and saving no one. But after a while, I started to understand. It was a moral thing. Fighting an enemy with dead bodies all around wasn't a confidence builder. It was the same with the wounded. They knew that if they were injured, we would come and fly them back to medical care. We weren't the most popular people when we were taking them into a firefight, but when we were there to get them out, that was another story. We were their best friends when we flew in supplies, ammunition, food, and medical aid.

We flew Lurps... Long Range Reconnaissance teams, Priests, and Chaplains, we flew Command and Control missions for Commanding Officers so they could watch their people from above. We were spotters for artillery. We were even asked to fly low and slow; we were trying to draw fire so they could spot enemy positions. I didn't overthink that one, myself.

Once we were fired at, we circled back over that area and dropped smoke grenades, marking their position. Our gunships would take it from there. Yes, gunships were an essential part of the Assault Helicopter Company. They liked to think it was named after them.

Then, there were the missions that everyone hated. Flying in Lurps (LRRPs) was one of the worst. Not because we didn't like Lurps, but because the ship that dropped them off was the one that had to extract them if they made contact. They always made contact.

Lurps had testicles the size of cantaloupes. These guys were fearless. Their job, as I understood, was to go in and find the enemy and report back. Recon work. Their job, as they saw it, was to engage large companies of VC or NVA soldiers with their six-man team using hit-and-run tactics. Or ambushes. Lurps were young and full of piss and vinegar. All the Lurp missions that I was involved in ended poorly. And we always got shot up pulling them out.

The other mission that sucked was the sniffer mission. Two things produce ammonia in their urine. Monkeys and humans. Our job was to fly low and slow over double or triple-growth jungle canopies with a large "hose" under the cargo area. We were trying to detect ammonia. Most of these missions were on the slopes of the mountains.

Updrafts and downdrafts would suck you under in a heartbeat. Just the fact that you had to fly low and slow made you a target. Our company lost two helicopters flying sniffer missions in the first month that we existed.

Plus, I wish I had a dollar for every monkey we killed in Vietnam. There were a crapload more monkeys in those mountains than there were VC. Don't misunderstand; there were plenty of VC, but nowhere near as many as monkeys.

Chapter 9: January 30, 1968

Our first missions as new Pilots weren't always challenging. "Today, you will be flying an advisor .... (fill in the blank).... to some of the outlaying Firebases. Try to keep him out of trouble. He likes to talk Pilots into taking him into hot landing zones. Don't do it. The last thing we need is to get one of you guys killed or lose a chopper.

He will want you to fly to several different LZs. He'll stay at each LZ for as long as it takes him to do what is needed. Just go where he tells you. It'll be a good opportunity for you to find some of the more remote LZs and Firebases. If you can't find them on your maps, don't worry, he'll tell you how to get there.

Then, add them to your maps. He makes this run once or twice every month."

Paraphrased, this would have been a typical briefing.

We called sorties like this "milk runs." During the first few weeks, these were pretty typical missions. "Today, we need you to fly to Phu Cat and pick up parts for 173. After that, we need to get 173 back in the air." Or "Today the Colonel needs someone to fly him around so he can inspect Bla bla bla..." Milk runs. Missions that put you to sleep. Missions that caused me to start believing, "This isn't going to be all that bad." But I kept hearing stories about other units and some of the missions they were getting and thinking about how lucky I was to be with the 61st AHC. The Lucky Stars, indeed. We were learning how to get around, and we were being watched. As soon as we were ready, we started receiving actual missions.

Around the end of my fourth week, I was greeted with my first real mission. That morning's briefing was short and to the point. I would be flying a Special Forces Lieutenant, two Special Forces Sergeants, and one Vietnamese interpreter to a small village 35 klicks or kilometers north of Qui Nhon Air Base. A village too small to be named on our map. It was little more than a group of farmers living in the middle of a patchwork of rice paddies and dikes. From 3,000 feet, it reminded me of a giant checkerboard. The patties were, more or less, square and surrounded by earthen dikes, all of which were wide enough for a man to walk down or a little wider. Occasionally, you would see one that was wider than the others. I guessed that those were their equivalent of a road. Dikes like these were used to move farm animals, primarily ducks, pigs, and water buffalo, and to travel to and from markets. Occasionally, you'd see a motorcycle or a scooter zipping across one of these dikes. Still, more often than not, it would be a simple hand cart loaded with whatever they were moving that day. I found out later that some of these carts carried more than produce.

Although I had only flown a few missions, sorties as we called them, I had flown over this village several times. Our area of responsibility was north of Qui Nhon. Most flights for our base either took us over or past it almost daily. There was a larger dry square in the middle of the patchwork. It was filled with trees, animals, and homes. Some of the houses were more than the expected thatch hooches. They appeared to be made of mud brick or other more permanent material with tile roofs and fenced yards. All of them were whitewashed. Not what I expected to see in the middle of a rice paddy. There were gardens and animal pens scattered between the houses, and most had at least one tree growing in the center of their yard. If I had taken a picture and sent it home, it would have been difficult to realize that it was a Vietnamese village in a country in the middle of a "civil" war.

Let me stop here and say this, I never considered this war civil. Not then, not now. There wasn't anything civil about what I saw that year. These people weren't fighting to keep their two countries separated. We were. This was only one of the many revelations I would discover the following year.

Again, I feel compelled to stop here and explain that parts of Vietnam were as beautiful as any place I have ever seen. Mountains with gentle grassy slopes slowly turning upward gave the impression that the land had been sculpted by the hand of some artist God. Jungles that were three canopies deep filled with the sounds of monkeys and birds and the occasional tiger. Streams were running down mountainsides almost any place you looked, especially from my vantage point, thousands of feet above the ground. Small lakes were sprinkled across almost every low point in the high mountains.

They had an ocean with water as clear as any you could find in the Mediterranean. They were as blue and clear as I remembered in Destin, Florida. Their beaches were so pristine and beautiful that if not for this war, they would have been in competition with any other country in the world for the tourist trade.

The only thing that may have been more beautiful than the beaches was flying into one of the old French villages high up in the mountains. The people there were well-educated, prosperous, and polite. Many of them spoke French as well as they spoke their own language. The food, aah, the food was as wonderful. But it was the beautiful ladies that graced the restaurants and shops up and down the streets that made these villages genuinely unique. Altogether,

Vietnam was beautiful. I could have made a fortune bringing tourists to those villages.

But for now, it was time to get down to business. Our passengers for the day had arrived. The Special Forces Lieutenant began his briefing almost as soon as we were airborne. The Lieutenant started by explaining that overnight, a company of North Vietnamese Army Regulars (NVA) had been seen crossing the rice paddies just north of the village. It was believed that they had stopped in the village to rest during the day. They had probably chosen that village to restock their food supplies because it was prosperous or maybe because the people there were sympathetic to their cause. The Lieutenant wasn't sure. I learned later that the village would be treated as hostiles when we were unsure. I remember someone saying it was better to be safe and alive than sorry and dead. The Lieutenant said that the NVA's ultimate destination was undoubtedly Qui Nhon. It was believed that they were part of the ongoing Tet Offensive. No one was sure. This was new ground for all of us. It was my first real mission. This one wasn't just a sortie.

A company of South Vietnamese soldiers (ARVN), along with their American advisers, had been flown in earlier that morning and had surrounded the village. The ARVNs had the NVA (North Vietnamese Regulars) soldiers pinned down. However, when we actually arrived, it was apparent that no one was sure who had who pinned down. The other thing was that the ARVN company commander couldn't be found. That was the real problem.

Circling overhead were U.S. jets ready to destroy the village. The only one authorized to issue that order was the missing ARVN Company Commander. Next, we learned that the jets had been there long enough that they were getting low on fuel. Someone needed to make a decision. Protocol dictated that it be the ARVN Captain, but soon, someone needed to step up and take charge.

We now knew why we were there. Our Special Forces team had been summoned to "determine the situation" and to find the ARVN Company Commander. Or... bomb the crap out of the village.

As we approached the village, the Lieutenant contacted one of the American advisers and started getting updates on the situation. The ARVN Company Commander had been found hiding under one of the hooches and was refusing to come out. Other than that little ditty, everything was as we had been advised. The good news, the village was surrounded. The bad news, both sides were taking heavy fire. We were about to fly into the middle of an active firefight, my first. As we approached the village, we could hear what they were referring to as "active." All hell had broken loose. It was active, alright.

As we approached the village, we started talking to the team leader on the ground. We asked them not to "pop smoke." Popping smoke was a way to mark the point that they wanted us to land. By watching that smoke, we could determine wind direction and speeds. It was the ground team's way of saying this was a safe place to land. But it also told the enemy where to line up their machine guns for those few magic seconds when we were just touching down before we could take off again.

Then, it all started going wrong. Someone popped smoke, even though we asked them not to. We were committed to the landing. We couldn't safely undo what we had committed to. Our passengers were already standing on the skids, ready to jump off and take cover. The ground team in front of us and below had the wounded ready to load. They were all committed and ready for us to touch and go.

We started taking heavy fire the second that we touched down.

I was riding the left seat that day. The more experienced Pilot sat in the right seat. He had been in country two or three weeks longer than me. He was the aircraft commander, and I was the co-pilot. Today, he sat between me and the incoming fire. It might have felt safer, but the truth was, it didn't make any difference. I could hear both AK rounds and fifty calibers firing in our direction. A fifty could easily pass through five men. We started taking rounds immediately.

I can only speak for myself here, but this was when time seemed to slow down. Everything was happening in slow motion. There was a clarity that I would feel several times again later. I could hear rounds passing in front of my face inside the cockpit. I could hear rounds hitting the chopper. It sounded like someone banging a baseball bat on a loosely covered snare drum. Each round sounded tinny but loud when they struck.

I could see the two Special Forces Sergeants diving into the rice paddy, trying to put the dike between them and the incoming fire. Then I saw the other Pilot's helmet give a quick little nod to my side and then back upright. An AK round ricocheted off his helmet and into the fuse panel above and between us. I heard more rounds whistling around me. All this time, I could hear the Crew Chief and Gunner behind me talking on the intercom. The Gunner was firing his M-60 non-stop. The Crew Chief was facing the opposite direction and could only wait until we took off again before he could get a shot off. Right now, his job was directing people on and off the aircraft and keeping watch on our open side.

Then I realized that the Vietnamese interpreter was still sitting inside the chopper directly behind me. He was talking on his PRC walkie-talkie. I turned and yelled for him to get out. He was looking at me and talking on his radio when, Poof, just like that, he was gone. There was a blast of red spray, and he disappeared. While I was yelling at him to get out, a fifty caliber round went through his radio and hit him in the side of his head. That red spray that I saw was his brains and blood.

He was there one second, and the next, he was gone. His seat belt was still attached but no longer wrapped around his waist. His boots were still sitting on the deck where his feet once were, but he was gone. All that was left was the red spray on the top of the cabin, around the left rear door, and on the floor. I was looking at him and yelling for him to get out, and a split second later... he was gone.

One of the Sergeants was climbing back on board, and I could see that he was bleeding from his foot or ankle. I couldn't tell which. Blood was bubbling up at the top of his boot. The other sergeant was helping him get in. At this point, I had no idea where the Lieutenant was. I can only assume he was there doing what he was sent to do. The last time I saw him, he had just jumped out the left side of the chopper into the rice paddy. A few seconds later, I saw him climbing up the side of the dike toward the battle. I don't know where he went after that.

Then I saw the Gunner helping the Crew Chief. He was standing over him, holding him upright, and trying to talk to him over the intercom. It looked like he was trying to determine if he was still alive. Then I heard the Gunner say that it looked like the Crew Chief had taken a shotgun blast in the middle of his back... dead center. Then, two more wounded were either put on board or made it on their own. I didn't see which. But what I did see next was the blood coming through my Gunner's shirt on the right side. He had been hit. Judging by the blood, I guessed he was hit before he stopped to help the Crew Chief. He was still trying to help the other wounded people on board. He kept shuffling between the Crew Chief and the passengers.

Then I heard the Special Forces sergeant yell, "Get the hell out of here." I looked back in the cabin again and realized that people had finally stopped getting on and off the aircraft. At that point, either the right seat Pilot or I, I don't remember which, started pulling in pitch, rolling the nose forward, and taking off. Even then, or I should say, especially then, I could hear rounds hitting the aircraft. More now than before. They made that odd tinny thud over and over until we were finally in the air and flying out of range. We started circling around and away from the village. I could see holes everywhere. Then came the smell of JP4. (Jet fuel) We were losing fuel even though our fuel bladders were self-sealing. Maybe they were self-sealing if we were being hit by AK rounds, but I don't think they were designed to withstand a fifty caliber. They were leaking, just leaking, not spewing. We ignored it. We could deal with that later. We had a more pressing problem now.

The Gunner was moving around the cabin. He was helping each of the wounded and then reporting to us what condition each of them was in. He put a tourniquet on the Special Forces Sergeant's leg and tried to slow the bleeding. The Sergeant was sitting in a puddle of his own blood. Then, the Gunner almost whispered over the intercom and said that the Crew Chief was still alive but unconscious. "He looks bad." I could tell he didn't want to state the obvious. They were friends.

Having friends was one of the things that I learned wasn't good. Losing a friend was much worse than losing a fellow Pilot or Crew Chief. That was my next great revelation. Having a friend or two was unavoidable, but it was stupid to look for new friends. People needed a lot of friends in the real world, but not here.

Now the big question for me and the other Pilot was whether we should tempt fate and try to fly back. Several gauges were not working. We didn't have any idea what condition our chopper was in. It could have been from the AK round that hit the overhead console, or it could be telling us we had a bigger problem. We didn't know which. The gauge that we were most concerned about was the one showing zero oil pressure in our transmission.

If we landed, we could expect another chopper to pick us up in as little as thirty minutes, if we were lucky, maybe less. But the Gunner was telling us that the Crew Chief wouldn't make it if we did. To a man, we all chose to keep going and try to save the Crew Chief's life.

If the blades freeze up, well, a helicopter has the glide ratio of a rock when the blades stop turning. No one complained. No one suggested that we land and wait. I pushed the cyclic forward and stayed as close to the ground as possible. I'm not sure why I thought that mattered. At 125 knots, we would roll up into a ball the second we hit the ground. If the engine stopped, I could auto-rotate to the ground safely. If the blades seized, we were dead.

As we approached Qui Nhon Air Base, I made a radio call to the tower and declared an emergency. I requested a straight-in approach. They answered by asking us to approach from the East and land on runway bla bla, and they started giving us wind directions and asking us to watch for other aircraft... that's when I answered back. "Negative! Negative! We are carrying wounded and flying a damaged aircraft. Again, this is Lucky Star 514, and we are approaching from the North. Again, we are requesting a straight-in approach. We request an ambulance and fire truck meet us on the runway."

As you would expect any good air traffic controller to do, he told us to continue our approach. He immediately started rerouting all aircraft in the area. When we landed, a fire truck and an ambulance were waiting.

The minute we touched down, medics ran to our chopper and started working on the Crew Chief. Then, a second crew started pulling the other wounded off the chopper. After that, one medical team after another took our wounded until the other Pilot, and I was by ourselves. We stayed with the aircraft so that we could keep the blades turning, trying to keep the fumes from catching fire. That part might have been stupid. I don't know if it helped, but as the last ambulance pulled away, the blades sieged. We jumped out and ran, and the fire truck started foaming the chopper down.

Here's the odd part. I remember almost everything that happened that day, as if it was yesterday, except for what happened next. We stood around for what seemed like forever, but it was probably no more than fifteen or twenty minutes. Then, a chopper from our company showed up to give us a ride. We were flown back to Camp Lane and told that we needed to fill out an incident report or some other damned report. To be honest, I don't remember which. When we finally finished filling out paperwork and telling our story, I heard someone say that he was putting us in for a bronze star. I don't think either of us was impressed. We just wanted to get back to our quarters and clean up. I felt dirty. I wanted to clean the blood from my face and clothes. There wasn't much, just a few droplets, but it felt dirty. I didn't want a medal. I wanted a bath.

A few days later, we were told that 14 rounds went through the fuel bladder, and a bunch more hit the aircraft's structure. They said that they were amazed that we had survived. I told them that I was too. Amazed, that is. When I think back, it was the Gunner who should have been given the Bronze Star, not we two Pilots. Because he kept firing, the NVA were probably firing at him, not us. We would have been easy targets if they hadn't been dodging his fire. I believe he saved all our lives. (If you are reading this, thank you.)

By the way, I never heard anything about a bronze star after that day, for the door gunner or us. I still believe the door gunner was the man of the day.

The Crew Chief was medivaced out of country that same day. I don't know if he survived or not. The Sergeant was taken to the hospital. Since he wasn't part of our unit. I don't know if he lost his foot.

The Gunner's wound was a clean "in and out" shot through the fatty tissue just above his belt line on his right side. Who says having a spare tire is bad for you? He was back a couple days later, a little sore but none the worse for wear. Not one of us that I am aware of, ever talked about it again. We didn't dwell on spilled milk back then. I'm not sure why. Maybe living through it once was enough. Later that night at the officer's club, I discovered the benefits of good liquor. That would become another of the lessons that I learned that day. I didn't say that every lesson that I learned was good.

After that day, I stopped trying to remember people's names. If you told me I would fly with Warrant Officer Jones or Smith the next day, I would know who you were talking about. But I didn't want to "know" who you were talking about. It just wasn't healthy. That was part of the process of separating yourself from the grief that comes from losing a good friend.

I've had people ask me about friends in Vietnam. We were soldiers. We were risking our lives every day to help each other. How much closer bond could you ask for? I didn't care if they were from Montana or Florida. I wanted to know they had my back and let them know I had theirs.

Note of interest: Online, I found one reference to this event. Searching "61st Assault Helicopter Company – History by Year, 1967 – 1968." I found the following quote. "One slick took rounds wounding the Crew Chief and Gunner: The Gunner was able to return to duty, but the Crew Chief was evacuated out of country."

Our government didn't want you to know what was happening in Vietnam. There is no other way to explain that entry in the company log.

As for me, "I swear before God Himself that the account above is accurate in every detail, as best as my memory allows." Trust me, you don't forget days like this one easily.

Reference material follows. This is as good a time as any for me to point out that, unlike the Viet Cong (VC), the NVA troops were well-trained, highly disciplined, and usually well-equipped. The ARVN soldiers were well-equipped but easily swayed and often undisciplined. The Viet Cong were a combination of both. Most VC soldiers were dedicated to their cause, which involved getting all foreigners out of Vietnam. They wanted to end a war that had been going on in one form or another for hundreds of years. The VCs were poorly equipped and resorted to homemade weapons as often as necessary to stop what they called the aggressors. For them, one invader would leave, and immediately, another would take its place. As the war continued, their numbers grew. Farmers by day, soldiers by night.

That was the second significant discovery that I made that day. You never knew whose side that farmer was on. Most just wanted to farm their land and feed their families, but not all of them. Probably, more than we realized were VC or, at the very least, sympathetic to their cause.

Most of the people in power in Vietnam were getting rich, supporting whichever country was the invader that year. Whether the French this year or the Americans replacing the French made no difference to these people. They didn't care who delivered it as long as it was fresh money. As a result, half of South Vietnam was being run by politicians who cared little or nothing about the welfare of their people. The other half was the black-market dealers and the madams who had grown rich long before and were now rising to power. South Vietnam was a country run by crooked politicians and whores. These people were happy to see the new conquering forces arrive...

so long as we arrived with unlimited supplies of money, they could continue to prosper.

On the other hand, the villagers and farmers had heard all these promises. They were tired of trying to feed their families rice soaked in empty promises. These people were tired of their villages being destroyed by both sides. Vietnam was divided into so many pieces that not even our great American Armies could put it back together again. It took me all of four weeks to figure that out. That was my third revelation.

Why did the South Vietnamese people let us stay? First, for all the reasons above. Plus, most of them were starving, and when we arrived, we offered them fresh promises and new jobs. We let them cook for us and clean our laundry. We provided fresh young troops to patronize their bars and their brothels. They built our outhouses and kept the grass cut between our barracks and the fences that protected us. When they did all this, they measured the distances between those fences and our airfields and barracks. Then, they passed that information on to the Viet Cong so that their mortars would not be wasted trying to determine where to send them. They knew our schedules and our weaknesses. They even knew where not to waste their time. They often knew where we would fight the next day and when we planned to arrive.

Hooch maids were in front of us every day, and soon, we no longer saw them standing there. They were invisible to us. We talked about what we did that day and what we planned to do tomorrow in front of them. They never listened to anything we asked them to do. You could ask them to clean something, and they would ignore you.

We damn sure didn't tell them how much we appreciated their work. We were rude, and they were rude back to us. Soon, we learned to just ignore them. They were the flies on our walls. They cleaned our offices, they made our beds, and we paid them almost nothing because it was more than what they could make at home. We thought that they should be thankful that we were there. We believed that we Americans were great fighters and brave soldiers. They only saw lazy men who wanted them to do all our work.

Chapter 10: "Lurps" Part One

The most dreaded missions that I flew in Vietnam were the ones that involved transporting Lurps. On the one hand, they were the most exciting missions I flew. On the other hand, flying long-range reconnaissance patrol missions was as dangerous as anything we did. That said, they were never boring.

Flying LRRPs, known as Lurps, usually meant flying long hours over heavily infested areas, picking out a perfect landing spot. It didn't have to be an easy place to pick up troops. It had to be a place we could fly into, be out of sight for six seconds, and fly out.

During those six seconds, six troops would jump out of the helicopter, hopefully unseen, without the aircraft ever coming to a complete stop. Inserting Lurps was, in general, our fun mission. If their mission went well, they were fun to recover. Note: The aircraft and crew that flew them in were the aircraft and crew that would extract them. It was that simple.

Before I get started here, I want to say this. I have the utmost respect for the bravery and abilities of all the men who volunteered to become Lurps. I wouldn't want to do what they did. Most of them felt the same way about helicopter pilots. But we pilots thought the Lurps were exposing themselves to more danger than they should have. We each were doing what we loved. Their name suggested that they were there to collect reconnaissance. They thought that they were there to create havoc. The differences between Lurps and Pilots were simple. When they got in trouble, we were called to get them out. We went into harm's way to take them out of harm's way.

That didn't make us better, but it didn't make us the same. The most difficult missions that I flew almost always involved Lurps. In fact, the worst mission that I ever flew involved extracting a Lurp team. I respected them, but I feared the possibilities of each Lurp mission more than any other sortie. It was the perfect love-hate relationship.

A Lurp team usually consisted of six heavily armed troops inserted into an enemy area to gather critical information for future use. In other words, they were scouts sent into possible hostile territory to reconnoiter enemy strengths and positions. Their mission was to get in, find out as much as possible, and get out without detection. If they were detected, it would sound all sorts of alarms for the enemy troops they were supposed to report back on.

The enemy needed stealth to remain capable of moving, setting up for their next contact, and resting, just like any other guerrilla combat group. If they were located, they had to move again and find a new location to initiate their next attack. It also meant that we had to locate them again. That meant starting over again on both sides. If we knew where they were, we could follow them and attack them when we were ready.

Lurps were there to find them and gather troop strengths and locations, not start a battle. They were supposed to slip in and out without detection. (One of the r's in their name stood for recognizance.) Then return to base camp and report their findings. Then, we had options. We could call in airstrikes, move our troops into blocking positions, or simply prepare for the inevitable. The problem with this mission plan? That's not how the Lurps saw their missions.

To complicate the situation, enemy troops sent their equivalences to Lurps in scouting teams. Unlike our

Lurps, these teams worked close to their main body. They were there to ensure that our Lurps didn't find their people. Each side could set up ambushes. The problem for our side was simple. By contacting enemy scouts, we alerted the enemy's main body that we were there and knew where they were. Everyone who survived had to find a new hiding place and start over. Good for their side, bad for our side. Plus, we must remember that they had radios like we did. If our Lurps were detected, it might take an hour or more for help to arrive. If NVA scouts called for help, it usually only took a few minutes for help to arrive.

It sounds so simple when I say it like that. I could never figure out why the Lurps had difficulty understanding that.

Inserting Lurps was usually a two-day event. The first day was our chance to do practice runs and find acceptable drop points. This might have been related to the fact that we were new at this process as Pilots. Remember, we were new units, and almost everything we did was a first for us.

This is secondhand knowledge, but I was told that Lurps had to hike in and back out before choppers arrived. And as you would guess, the information they brought back was dated before it could be used. Being "choppered in" sped up that process considerably. They could return to their base camps with locations and troop strengths that were current. They could be extracted one day, and on that same day, more troops could be choppered back in, or more likely, we could bomb the hell out of the enemy and then return and mop up.

This morning began with four choppers flying out to the area that the Lurps wanted to scout. The first chopper was the Command and Control bird, carrying the ranking officer to supervise and direct the exercise. This C and C chopper usually flew at 3,000 plus feet. The three remaining choppers were there to find a suitable drop point. We spent most of our time flying low and slow. Each chopper had a predetermined but approximate area to look for a practical insertion point. These sites were spread out so the enemy could not see which chopper had dropped the Lurps off. Our passengers and the crew would look for high points with good cover. Maybe I should just explain my flight and not try to talk about the other two. All three choppers had the same objective. When inserting the Lurps, only one chopper would have troops on board.

We were looking for high ground and good cover to drop our team without them being seen exiting the chopper. On that mission, we found a depression at the top of a hill with high grasses and a tree line probably forty or fifty yards from where we planned to drop them. We flew over to the spot that we had chosen and looked at it as best we could without drawing any more attention than we had to. We were looking for a point where we could fly in, disappear for six or seven seconds, and reappear, coming out of the depression. Just enough time to flare... raise the nose of the chopper and slow down enough that our team could jump out, and then nose the chopper over and fly out of the depression. We were looking for a blind spot that would allow approximately six seconds for the team to jump out of the chopper without the chopper ever setting down. In other words, we needed to fly low and slow enough that they could jump out without breaking any body parts. Remember, these men were traveling light, but they were heavily armed. Other than a change of socks and a few modest rations, any extra weight was mostly arms and munitions. Did I mention that they were heavily armed?

Command and Control's job was to observe each of the three choppers fly in and out of their site, one at a time. Then decided which chopper would be the best suited to drop the Lurps the following day. When I flew in, the C and C chopper lost sight of us for maybe ten seconds and then saw us come out the other side. We were golden. Without knowing it, I had just drawn the short straw. I would be the chopper that inserted the Lurps the next day.... Which also meant I would be the guy that came back and picked them up when they were ready to leave.

We weren't told which chopper would carry the Lurps until the next day. The same four helicopters and crews from the previous day were ready for us the next morning. We were going to repeat the exercise, except this time, we were dropping the Lurps off. When the Lurps started loading on my helicopter, I pretty much figured it out all by myself.

Today's mission varied from the previous day's operation in two respects. The first variation was that one of us had Lurps aboard. The second was that all three choppers would hit our drop points in unison. Then, in and out and return to base.

The other three choppers were assigned new sorties, and the drop chopper was given milk runs. Always close to our pickup site. Pick up site? The extraction site will be wherever they were when they needed to leave. When? As long as it took. Usually, two or three days, sometimes more. At this point, we waited. We always stayed busy but always close by.

Chapter 11: The Brothers Grimm

You need to read this chapter before you try to figure out why I gave it the title. Some stories are like onions and have more than one layer. This is not a bedtime story for children. I'll leave it to you to peel this onion. It's not that complicated.

There was a small village outside Dong Ba Thin Base where I was stationed. For the location, think 25 miles northwest of Cam Ranh Bay Air Force Base and one mile from the Dong Ba Thin Annex. Most of the people in this village either worked at Dong Ba Thin for the military or had relatives who did. A few performed services for the Camp that did not actually work on the base. Use those who performed laundry services as an example. But, the majority of the villagers worked in the Camp. They performed duties like the mamasans who cleaned our hooches and took our laundry back to their village. I'm not sure who washed our clothes. I know they boiled down fish scales to make the starch they used. Unfortunately, I know that for all the wrong reasons.

There were cooks, carpenters, dishwashers, and most importantly, the "Honey Pot" men, as we called them. They were the guys who loaded and unloaded the fifty-five-gallon drums that were cut in half and placed under the latrines... outhouses.

They were infamous for pulling them out while someone was sitting above. Once out and away from the outhouse, they poured diesel fuel over the contents and set them afire. It was the military's way of waste disposal. It was not the best job in the camp, but it was the most sought-after job due to the pay scale. We offered the locals many such job opportunities. So, the local resentment was understandable.

One other job opportunity was making charcoal. This village excelled in making charcoal. Little dome ovens lined the road running from our camp through the village. Frequently, parts of the road were covered with dense smoke from the kilns. It was a lot like trying to drive through California during a drought.

The charcoal was used by the locals to cook with, but more important to us, it was used when we cooked out or had a barbecue. This little village had its own cottage industry, making charcoal from our scraps, ammo boxes, and end pieces from construction. Still, primarily, they used broken pallets from the Camp. Everything we received came on a pallet. We had a regular recycling center right next to the Camp. We were years ahead of the U.S.

A quick note here. I'm unsure whether to call Dong Ba Thin a Camp or a Base. We were attached to Cam Ranh AFB for logistics, but Dong Ba Thin was initially an Army Engineering Camp. Later, it became the 10th Combat Aviation Battalion Headquarters. So it was called, at least when I was there, a base by one group and a camp by the other. It doesn't matter. I tell you this so that you know they were in the same place.

This story started one day when two American soldiers drove through that village in an Army deuce and a half truck. (Two-and-a-half-ton heavy-duty truck) Some villagers say that the soldiers were high. Others said that they were just stupid. The problem was that they didn't slow down when they drove through the smoke from the charcoal ovens. None of that mattered. They ran over and killed two Vietnamese locals squatting down in the middle of the road.

Why were they squatting in the middle of the main road? That's what Vietnamese people did. They squatted when they stopped to talk, rest, or just contemplate the world's affairs in general. Who knows?

Vietnamese weren't accustomed to vehicles traveling on their roads. They couldn't afford them. They used bicycles and ox carts, vehicles like that. However, the occasional military vehicle traveling on the road was a hazard that they were apparently willing to accept. Primarily because the U.S. Army Corp of Engineers built the highways so that their large trucks could travel safely.

When they met, they squatted and talked in the middle of the road. The road behind them was covered with smoke. Our two soldiers, who were either stupid or high, drove a two-and-a-half-ton military monster truck over the two squatters. As you would expect, it killed both of the squatters.

The villagers were outraged. Their village elder, or mayor or whatever they called him, went to the Army and demanded justice for the death of two of his citizens. He demanded reparations to his village for its losses and to the families of his two citizens. He asked for quite a bit more than they might have been able to make even if they lived another hundred years. His only other demand was that the two soldiers be arrested and charged immediately.

In the meantime, our investigators discovered that the two villagers were NVA soldiers. They also learned that they did not live in the village after all. In fact, they were forcing a local family to feed and house them. They were recovered from injuries sustained in a battle with U.S. soldiers just north of the village several months earlier.

When this new information was presented to the village elder, he allowed the Army to release the two soldiers, and the village awarded them with medals of valor for their services to the village. But the village never returned the reparations made to them.

The two soldiers went from zeros to heroes in one day. They got a write-up in the Stars and Stripes, the military equivalent of the New York Times newspaper, or some other big news outlet.

Chapter 12: Dear John

Today will be another milk run day. Our preflight briefing was short and to the point. Two choppers were needed to fly down to an airbase south of us and pick up the parts for our unit. I apologize for being vague here, but what we were doing that day is irrelevant to the story.

Two choppers were to fly south, following the coast to that base. We were taking the scenic and safe route. During that briefing, we were told that the base had been receiving small arms fire from the village next to it, and we would probably be asked to land from the ocean side. As an extra precaution, we were told that even though we were only going to be there for an hour or so, we needed to be sure we parked in the revetment area for choppers. This was due to the enemy sniper fire from the nearby village and the fear of a possible mortar attack.

For those not in the military, revetments are "L" shaped walls that protect aircraft from incoming mortars or artillery and the resulting fires from the JP4. Picture having a wall on one side and in front but open on the opposite side and back. They are designed for choppers to get in and out of safely. And to protect on the blocked side but not on the open side. In other words, they were designed to save at least part of your fleet from incoming rounds. In theory, it was supposed to protect enough of your inventory that you could carry out a retaliatory action later.

When we announced that we were in the Base's air space, we were instructed to land from the waterside, as expected, and to avoid flying over land near the base. This is because the Base had small arms fire from the village next to the base. Later, we learned that they wanted to maintain a good relationship with the people in that village and not have to destroy it.

They said that they were working on a remedy as they spoke. Which probably meant that they had a team working their way through the village trying to locate the sniper. We were advised to land at our convenience from the East on runway 91. There were no other aircraft in the area. Aircraft usually took off over the water, giving the added advantage of headwinds on take-off. Coming from the waterside meant we would have tailwinds.

The problem they just gave us was landing with 20 to 30-knot tailwinds. If you can avoid it, you just don't do that with a chopper. Side winds, maybe, tailwinds never, and headwinds always when available. A chopper turns into a bucking bronco with tailwinds. Our solution was to land sideways. A chopper can fly in any direction you tilt your rotors. From a hover, push your cyclic left, and you fly left. Pull back and fly backward.

As we started our approach, we also started turning slowly around but still maintaining our glide path. Picture flying down a string running at a 45-degree angle. Now, do it again sideways. It would still be a tricky landing, but it is much less than having a tailwind.

The tower gave us a few compliments on our landing and informed us that there would be a pick-up truck in front of us shortly with a "Follow Me" sign. The truck would escort us to the revetment and parking area. We hovered sideways down the runway and behind the pickup until it turned. We nosed it forward and continued following. We put on quite a show for the jet jockeys. I don't think their jet pilots could be quite so resourceful. Maybe? I don't know, but this was an everyday thing for Army Pilots. Landing in jungle LZ's small enough that you couldn't turn around was not out of the realm of possibilities. Having to take off to one side or the other was expected. We didn't think of it as showing off. We felt that it was the way everyone did it.

Once we arrived at our parking spaces, our escort left us to park and go about our business. We parked in adjoining revetments and started our shutdown procedures. The Crew Chief and Gunner jumped out and began securing the aircraft.

I looked to my left and saw one of the Pilots from the other chopper walking away with his head down. He was looking at a sheet of paper. Prop wash was making it difficult for him to hold it. He was still wearing his flight helmet, and his visor was still down. Both of those things were wrong. He was outside his aircraft and needed to hear and see what was happening around him.

He walked over to the revetment barrier wall and started climbing over. It happened so fast that no one could have stopped him. The blades on his chopper were still turning as he climbed to the top of the wall and stood upright. I believe that he thought he was below the reach of the blades. But, maybe his mind was elsewhere. I don't know how else it could have happened.

His body was slammed into his own aircraft. His crew ran to help, but there wasn't anything that they could have done. Finally, one of them ran after the paper he was reading and picked it up. He wanted to know what was so important that his pilot would give his life for it. Later, he showed us. His name was... I'm not going to do that. It was a goodbye letter from his fiancée, "Dear John, please forgive me, but I have fallen in love with.........."

He was a warrant officer fresh out of flight school. Someone told me later that he was maybe twenty years old. I will not use his real name because it doesn't matter. No one other than the guys in our company would have any idea how he died. The Army was kind in that respect. If someone died in less than an honorable manner or in an accident, they still sent a letter to his family, complimenting his bravery and devotion to duty.

It should be remembered that most of these soldiers were still teenagers, kids. They weren't mature adults who had been called on to risk their lives for their country. They were kids.

Some became leaders and rose to great heights, but a few could never get past being a teenager right out of high school. Some of those just got lost in the chaos. They just couldn't grow up fast enough. They were teenagers stuck in Vietnam, and there wasn't any way for them to get back home before their year was over, short of the obvious. I don't know if he knew that he was about to lose his life over a girl or if he was simply lost in thought. It doesn't matter. He was just as dead either way.

Chapter 12a: The Beach Run

By now, I had been in the country for a couple months and had settled into the routine of flying twelve to fifteen hours a day, seven days a week. Our company moved north to an area called Bong Son. Someone told us that it was called LZ English. I had heard that name used before, but I understood that it was an Aussie outpost and, later, where the First Cav was based for a short time.

That day, we went from a bed in a building to a cot in a tent, and it was hot. The first building we constructed was our command center. Next, we built the enlisted men's and officer's clubs. Enlisted first. The mess hall was in a tent. It remained in a tent for as long as I was there. The latrines and showers were in tents without covers. The floors were red clay. Later, someone added wooden pallets to the showers.

By the way, when I say us, I am referring to my company. I was never asked to build anything. One good thing about being a pilot was that we were too busy flying to jack around doing menial work.

Late afternoon, we received a call to help a squad of Army troops trapped on the beach. NVA soldiers had them pinned down behind a small sand mound that ran the length of the beach. They were greatly outnumbered, had been pinned down for several hours, and were running out of ammunition. They were trying to keep the NVA from rushing their position before help arrived. That's assuming that you could call a sand berm a defensive position. The NVA knew they would run out of munitions soon and could simply walk in and take their position without significant casualties.

Our instructions were to return to the base, and while we refueled, they would load our chopper with ammunition. Their final message said it all. "If you can get there before dark, these guys might make it out alive. If not, I don't think they will. It will be difficult to find them after dark."

Dark in Vietnam is black. There are no streetlights, fires, or lights in windows. In Vietnam, these would all be signals that someone was up to something. Lights in Vietnam were targets for both sides. Dark is dark in Vietnam, especially if it is cloudy, which was the case most often. If there was no moon to help light your way, flying over a white beach doesn't help either. I worked one winter in a uranium mine in Colorado, the Schwartzwalder mine, owned by the Cotter Corporation. Working five hundred feet below ground without light is pitch black. It's holding your hand in front of your face and not seeing it. There was little difference between Vietnam on a dark night and that mine... or the inside of my chopper. Turning on your cockpit, lights blinded you when it was that dark. Turning on your spotlight made you a target. The white beach sand helped very little. Black was black, no matter what color the ground below was.

We were assigned an area between the mountains and the beach that day. That meant we were the closest. Having to refuel and load up with ammo slowed us down, but not to the point that we would not be able to make it before dark-dark if we hurried. If we found them soon enough, once we arrived. Finding people was always a challenge since there were no street signs.

The base called us again at the last minute and told us they were adding troops to our load. We were going to drop troops behind the NVA and then fly down the beach and push out supplies and ammunition behind our guys. Now, it sounded more like a plan. An imperfect plan, maybe, but at least it was a plan.

We needed to load as many troops as possible and leave room for the ammunition. The problem we were making for ourselves was the weight we were trying to take off with. We were in the middle of summer, and it was hot. We went through a couple weeks in Vietnam when it never got below 100 degrees, even after dark. That kind of moist, hot air does not offer a chopper the lift that cold air does. Our first attempt at taking off was not successful. We were grossly overloaded.

We had a brand-new metal runway with a gradual drop-off at the end. This time we would try to gather enough ground speed and forward air passing through the blades that we might be able to start climbing before we reached the end of the metal runway. If we could get enough speed before we crossed the end of the runway and as we crossed over the drop-off, we might be going fast enough to continue climbing.

We were maxed out by the end of the runway. As we approached the drop, I gently pulled back on the cyclic and added more lift to our forward speed. We lifted maybe five feet, but five feet was enough for me to pick up more airspeed because we were no longer sliding on our skids down the runway. Less friction gave us more speed. More speed offered less drag. We were flying and climbing. I finally heard someone in the back talking. It was the first sound other than the chopper since we told them what we were trying to do. "Oh, ye of little faith."

To this day, I'm not sure why I thought we could do what we did. The only answer I could come up with, other than stupidity, was that no one said, "Hey, we're not going to make it," so we kept going.

We did make it to the beach, and we arrived before it was too dark to do what we came to do.

First, we offloaded the troops. That lightened our load enough that we could maneuver well enough to carry out our plan. Now, the problem was the NVA was shooting at us too. The troops we dropped off started firing at the NVA and distracting them. As we flew along the beach, we radioed for the troops we were there to resupply. We asked them to shine their flashlights behind their berm. We needed to see the beach as we approached. We were trying to fly as close to the sand as possible. We warned them not to shine their flashlights in our faces. "Light up the ground," we asked. By this time, the NVA were primarily fighting the troops behind them. Their problem was trying to find cover for their front and rear simultaneously.

Only a few NVAs were firing toward the beach. I think they realized what we were doing.

We reached an airspeed in the neighborhood of forty knots as we flew past the troops the first time. The Gunner started pushing out ammo boxes while the Crew Chief kept the NVA looking down. We circled around and over the water and back down the beach again, dropping the balance of the supplies and ammo boxes. We were done. Once again, we were flying down the beach in total darkness. We had made it.

No one asked for us to pick up the wounded. We talked for a few seconds on the radio, and they thanked us for helping, but they were too busy to say much else. Then, as we were leaving, we heard the Star Blazers telling us they were taking over. Star Blazers was our gunships.

We gave them a clear description of the location. I assume that they sprayed the hell out of that beach. Gunships loved overkill. The NVA usually left as soon as they saw the Charlie models coming. Gunships were UH-1C's, or just Charlie models. We flew the

"H" models. They were better known as the slicks, taxis, or Cadillacs. I heard one guy say that they were station wagons. Most notably, the medivac choppers flew "H" models. There were a lot of names for slicks, but gunships were usually just called Charlie models, except for a few "frogs." Frogs were Charlies on steroids.

As with most of our missions, we rarely knew the outcome of our efforts. This wasn't due to callousness. We were busy. As soon as we finished one sortie, another was always waiting, except late at night. Nights were ours to rest, most of the time, but not always. But tonight, we were heading home and on our way to a hot meal, a shower, and some much-needed sleep. The Crew Chief and Gunner still had a hard night ahead of them. Their job was to perform any maintenance that our ship needed, and maintenance was always required. They could sleep in the chopper while we flew to our first mission in the morning. Unfortunately, most of their sleep came while we were in the air. It was the worst job in the Army if you ask me.

We knew they would do their best work. If we crashed and burnt, so did they. There was no greater confidence builder than knowing your mechanic was sitting behind you. It gave you that warm and fuzzy feeling you needed when you were being shot at. The Crew Chief and Gunner had the worst jobs in Vietnam. Yet they were always ready. They were the reason that we could do what we did.

No one ever complained about their crew chief and
gunner sleeping while we were flying at altitude.

Chapter 14: Free Falling

I knew we would be called upon to make a few "milk
runs" while we waited for the Lurps we had just
inserted to return, but I was still surprised by my next
mission. My morning briefing started with a warning.
Today, you will be flying Father Murphy to several
outlying landing zones, LZs. These were semi-
permanent sites where operations were conducted
away from the home base. I had heard most of their
names, but I hadn't flown to all of them.

"Your primary job will be to ensure the safety of
Father Murphy." If our job was keeping the good
Father safe, we would be safe. I liked that idea. I liked
it a lot.

Once a month, the Chaplain was flown around to
more remote units. He performed Mass for the
Catholics and accepted confessions. He offered
spiritual guidance to anyone who needed a few
minutes of sanity in a world gone mad, Catholic or
not.

By the way, I'm not using his real name here.
Father Murphy looked, in every way, like an Irish

Priest. He was a diminutive little man in stature, not character, topping out at maybe 5 feet tall. He pushed his Irish brogue just a little more than necessary. I think he was trying to add to the image of his calling. He had round red cheeks and a full belly, looking, for all the world, more like Santa Clause without a beard than a priest. He was even jolly. My immediate impression of the man was that he was proud of his image, heritage, and calling. He was every inch an Irish priest, but he had one glaring flaw. He wanted to see some action. My job that day was to ensure that he did not.

During the hour-and-a-half flight to our first stop, Father Murphy explained that he had always dreamed of performing the "Last Rites" in a battlefield setting. My first thought was that I needed to be sure he didn't perform them for me. Then he asked if we might just fly by a battle somewhere. Maybe they would need him.

After a while, I think he was finally starting to understand that we weren't going to take him anywhere near a battlefield, and he changed his approach. He explained that being tested by battle would make him a better priest. It might help him understand what his parishioners felt. Finally, in a desperate move, he admitted that he wanted bragging rights with the others in his profession. I wasn't sure if he meant when he returned to the States or if he meant here in Vietnam. The truth was, I had my orders and a will to live, and I wasn't swayed by any of his arguments. If anything, I stayed closer to the coast than I should have during our flight to Firebase Meade.

Meade was near the top of Two Corp, usually shown in Roman numerals. II Corp was near the top end of our working area and West of the coast. The upper part of Two Corp was mostly jungle-covered mountains except for the strip we followed today. A narrow strip of flat land composed of small farms, smaller villages, rice patties, and, on the outer edge, some of the most beautiful beaches in Vietnam.

Firebases were usually placed on the highest point in the area. Then, the tops were leveled as best they could and fortified with sandbags. Concertina wire was placed around the perimeter. All vegetation was cleared within 4 to 5 hundred yards of the perimeter. Sandbag hotels were created, and trenches were dug for cover. If a few trees weren't in the direction of fire, they were left for whatever shade and comfort they offered, but everything underneath them was cut down. The rest of the flat top was left open so the larger helicopters could perform their missions. First, earthmovers had to be brought to transform the mountain peaks into flat tops. Then, the choppers flew in the Howitzers needed at these firebases.

Firebase Meade had one distinctive feature. One side fell off almost straight down hundreds of feet to the valley below. Halfway down, it started a gentle slope out and away from the mountain. This will be important later in this story.

About halfway to Meade, Father Murphy pulled out the big guns. "God would be on our side," he told us. We couldn't argue with that one. If we had told him how many dead and wounded troops were wearing crosses and St. Christophers were flown out of firefights each day, we would have only pissed him off. So we held our tongues and returned to trying to find Firebase Meade.

After we arrived, Father Murphy went straight to work. I must admit that watching Father Murphy's work was inspiring. He prepared a full-on Mass by spreading white tablecloths and doilies over some ammo boxes, unfolding and laying them from rear to front on the altar. He placed a white runner with purple borders and a dove flying down toward the runner's tip. Then he dawned his vestments. First, a simple loose white tunic and then a white and purple yoke draped around his neck. Next, he added a small black cap to his head. Lastly, he set out a box of wafers and made his call to service. I apologize. I am not Catholic. I do not know the names of these garments, and I do not mean to offend any of you who are Catholic. What Father Murphy did in the middle of the jungle and on the top of a mountain was magical. I would have joined the Catholic Church on the spot if I had not already been baptized Mormon. I had no idea what a Mass was supposed to sound or look like, but what this Priest did that day was inspiring.

He followed his Mass with an out-of-the-way confessional area and took all comers, Catholic or not. That part was a little odd to me. I'm not sure I would have been comfortable telling God my deepest and darkest secrets sitting under a tree close to my buddies. Still, I knew that some of these guys needed absolution. Unfortunately, for some, there would never be enough "Hail Marys and Our Fathers" in their lifetime to help save their souls or quench their need to end their guilt. But Father Murphy tried.

As I watched Father Murphy work his magic, a plan began to form in my mind. It would take another hour for it to come together fully. Then, I needed to let my crew and the other Pilot know my plan. I wanted to give Father Murphy what he was seeking without scaring the hell out of my crew. Father Murphy wanted to satisfy his need to know what it felt like to be in harm's way. Soon, he would be able to appreciate what his parishioners felt when they described their fears. The more I thought about it, the better it sounded.

To give you, the reader, an appreciation of what I was about to do, I need to explain the dynamics of my plot. First, a helicopter creates an air cushion around and between itself and the ground while it hovers. Picture a circle of air coming through the blades. First, it hits the ground, then it is pulled back around and down through the blades again. Completely surrounding the body of the aircraft with an air cushion. Thus helping hold the aircraft above the ground. Like any fan, the blades are shaped to draw air down and thus create lift.

Second, the faster a helicopter falls, the faster the blades turn. That's how a helicopter makes an auto-rotation when it loses power. As you fall, the blades build up speed. As you approach the ground, you start building a ground cushion. There's more, but it's complicated. You flare to gather more forward air through the blades and begin to slow your descent... Bla bla bla.

When I detailed my plan to the crew, they were less enthusiastic but agreed to go along.

While waiting for Father Murphy to finish his services, I saw a Lurp team and their dog walking into camp. Service dogs are not pets. This dog was part of the team. These Lurps were there to rest, resupply, and probably get some sleep. I watched the dog and his handler. He fed his dog first, and then he ate. They both ate the same food, MRE rations. (Meals Ready to Eat)

When he lay down to rest, his dog lay next to him. The dog showed respect for his handler, and the handler showed equal respect for his dog. They were a team. That was obvious.

I had heard stories of soldiers who refused to leave Vietnam because they would not leave their dogs behind. This guy looked like he would be one of those that stayed.

It was time to leave. Everyone was excited to get back in the air. We were not used to staying in any place for more time than it took to drop off our passengers and cargo. We ensured Father Murphy was strapped in and wearing his helmet and had his headset plugged in. I wanted him to be able to hear us, and I especially wanted to be able to listen to him.

We went through our start-up procedure. When everyone was ready, both pilots turned and started complimenting Father Murphy on his services. Someone, maybe me, even asked if he offered services for the K9s as a joke. He didn't take it as a joke. He immediately started explaining all the prayers and blessings he had given to animals, especially K9s and their soldiers.

Then it began. I pointed to Father Murphy's helmet and asked if he could hear me? I asked him to make sure he depressed his mic when he spoke. Then I yelled, "Push the send button before you talk."

All this time, I was slowly pulling in pitch and power. I was making the chopper lighter and lighter on its skids. Then, finally, it began to slide forward toward the edge of the cliff. The closer to the cliff we got, the more animated the good father became. I showed concern for what he was trying to tell me, but I kept telling him to make sure his mic was plugged in and that he was pushing the button before he spoke. His hand gestures were getting wilder by the second as we slipped over the edge and started free-falling down the mountainside.

That's when the good Father started screaming and tried to jump out of the chopper but couldn't get his seat belts to release.

I was still telling him to push the button before he talked.

As we slid down the side of that mountain on a cushion of air, the good Father's language began to change from the Irish brogue of the Priest I knew before to a tapestry of profanity reminiscent of a drunken sailor.

Then it happened. My plan started coming together. We reached the speed we needed to smoothly fly away from the cliff with only a slight push forward of the cyclic. I turned my attention back to the front of the aircraft. I pushed gently pushed the cyclic forward and pulled in pitch. We gracefully sailed forward and stopped falling. I think that's when the good Father realized what I had done to him. He sat back in his seat, smiled, and said, "F**k you, you bastard!" without the slightest hint of an accent.

When we dropped the good Father off that evening, it was the last time I saw him. I think he had enough excitement to last a lifetime or until he left Vietnam for good. He had learned in one afternoon what it might have taken someone else a lifetime to learn. It is not exciting when you think you are about to die.

It's frightening. Frightening and exciting are not the same thing. He should have figured that out long before. Flying into a firefight probably wouldn't be on his "to-do list" tomorrow. But that was just a guess on my part. Who am I to be putting words in a Priest's mouth?

Chapter 15: Gin and Tonic

Every Tuesday before breakfast, we lined up to take a quinine pill for malaria prevention. An enlisted man handed you one pill, and an officer watched to be sure you swallowed it. Then, he made you open your mouth and show him it was gone. My problem was that the quinine pills caused an "upset stomach." At first, it was a mild case of diarrhea, but the longer I took them, the worse it got.

On Tuesday, during a mission, right after dropping off troops in a hot LZ, I had to get out of my chopper and wash up in a stream. Unfortunately, I had an absolutely dire case of the drizzling shits.

You can imagine the "shit" I took over that little mishap. When we returned to LZ English, I swore before God and anyone who could hear me that I would not take another quinine pill, no matter the punishment. Later that night, I was approached by the medic and told that if I drank one gin and tonic every night, he would give me credit for taking the pill. Tonic water is also known as quinine water.

It didn't take long for me to figure out three things about gin and tonics. First, I liked gin and tonic. It was tasty. Second, if one gin and tonic helped protect you from malaria, imagine how much protection three or four would give you. Third, I slept much better after drinking three or four gin and tonics than if I didn't.

Chapter 16: The Blood Crater Legend

Rumors were flying about a bomb crater filled with blood just north of LZ Uplift. There had been a hellacious battle in that area the day before. The fighting lasted just short of 20 hours between Company A of the 1st Battalion (Mechanized) and the 50th Regiment, 1st Cav unit, some soldiers, and an NVA unit that was reported to be regimental in size. The battle started between approximately fifty members of Company A, with nine APCs and the NVA Regiment. Then escalated into a major battle resulting in the loss of... some were saying more than one hundred U.S. troops were either killed or wounded and even more NVA.

Note: We weren't exactly sure how many of our guys were killed. The number kept going down every day after. Finally, one of the 61st AHC pilots reported that the "Silver Fox," as the 1/50th commander liked to call himself, told his crew that there were no casualties. We knew that was a lie.

Two gunships from the 61st AHC were involved, and both were damaged. Both had to return to camp for repairs, but none of the crew was injured.

One guy said that more than 100 NVA bodies were found the morning after, and none had weapons. This indicated that the NVA had been in and carried off any wounded and as many dead as they had time to move. Retrieving the weapons and wounded probably occupied most of the night and prevented the NVA from removing all the remaining bodies. Usually, porters were required to perform those services.

Rumors were that one of the B52s made a direct hit on an underground network of tunnels and bunkers filled with troops. Someone else said that it was a regimental headquarters and hospital. Finally, one guy said that the B52 made a direct hit on a command bunker, and the crater filled with the blood of troops killed in the blast. Thus, the blood crater's name.

It all meant that no one knew anything, and rumors were running wild. Although I did like the idea that the B52s made a direct hit on an NVA underground bunker. And that the red was blood. If that sounds harsh, don't forget what we were doing there.

Those were the rumors that I heard while I was there. Here is what I know now.

There was a large bomb crater just north of LZ Uplift that I flew over several times. People called it the "blood crater," and I understand why. It looked like it had filled with blood-red water while all the others were filling with foamy greenish-brown water. Odder yet, it seemed to be getting redder each time we flew over it in the days that followed.

The bombed area was just outside of LZ Uplift and right after going through the pass, so we were flying at a higher altitude than we usually flew. Some of our guys said they could see bodies floating in the water. At that altitude, I couldn't see well enough to argue one way or the other.

The craters were a result of the high-altitude bombing attack by B52s during a multi-unit battle that had taken place in the nearby mountain valley. The battle had spilled over and down into that area. In a later briefing, we were told that an NVA Battalion had been operating in the area. They were probably headquartered someplace in the caves and tunnels found in the mountains surrounding LZ Uplift and in the pass leading into the bombed area. It was later determined that this area had a hospital complex, a rest and recuperation center, and an operational headquarters for the NVA.

The 61st AHC, along with several other airmobile units and a large multi-national troop force, had all worked together in this same engagement. But in the valley on the other side of the mountains. Our forces swept up the entire width of the valley and into the mouth of the valley. That caused some NVA troops to cross into the area near LZ Uplift. This probably led to the subsequent battles near LZ Uplift and the high-altitude bombings that followed.

I was part of that multi-unit task force that ferried troops into that valley, so I understand why there was so much confusion. Other than a few of our gunships, most of the 61st were involved on the other side of the mountain range while all this was happening.

A check online also answered the question of what caused the blood crater. One of the APCs involved in the battle that day drove into that crater and then couldn't get out and lost its transmission. So, the blood that was coating the water was transmission fluid. That's why it never changed color after so many days in the sun. That also explained why there was so much of it. It was a thin coating of transmission fluid, not a crater filled with blood. There was nothing spiritual or mystical about it. It was just transmission fluid.

Now, here's why I added this story to this book. I have heard several accounts from different people asking me if I ever saw the famous blood crater? Most of these guys were Vietnam veterans. The questions started when I told them I had and confirmed that it existed. Was it a direct hit on an underground city?

Did the locals throw their dead into the crater, thinking it was a sacred burial spot?

I could only tell them I didn't know the answers to their questions.

This story was exciting and mystical. It was the very heart of the stuff that a good war story is made of. But it was a war story. It wasn't real. Some guys will read this and think I am just trying to piss in their Wheaties. Look it up, guys. It was transmission fluid. My guess is that most of the stories you have heard were also War Stories.

Chapter 17: You Can't Stop Stupid

I'm not sure how to start this short story. I'm calling it a short story because it's a story that I have a problem dealing with. I want it to be brief. I have added it because it needs to be told for you to understand what was happening in Vietnam then.

We had a drug problem there. People came from the States, where the culture was changing, and drug use was becoming more common. New troops were bringing this new culture into the military. In retrospect, I think that I understand it now better than I did then. But understanding it and dealing with the deaths caused are two different things.

It helped the "newbies" cope with the shock of what they were being asked to do. It helped dull their senses when they saw things that were best left unseen. But the first few days in country were a shock to most of us. That wasn't a good excuse for their actions.

It was stupid, at best. First and foremost, your survival in Vietnam depended on being alert and aware of what was happening around you. Staying vigilant and getting high weren't compatible.

I will admit this story is an extreme situation, but it's true nonetheless. Unfortunately, a bunch of kids stoned out of their gourds made this story possible.

I have mentioned several times that most of the soldiers in Vietnam were teenagers. This was especially true regarding grunts, foot soldiers, and marines. Most of them joined the military right out of high school. They spent a couple months in boot camp and a few more months in rifleman training and then went straight to Vietnam. So having an eighteen- or nineteen-year-old soldier in your chopper wasn't unusual. I would guess that most of them were still in their teens. Some of them grew up fast and survived. Others, not so much. And there were always those who were not the brightest in their classes and never finished school. For them, the military was their only option. If that sounds harsh, wait until you read this and then decide.

We were flying between locations when we heard a call on the emergency channel. It asked if any choppers were in the area along a highway between two small villages. The names of the villages and the highways aren't relevant to this story, so I'll skip that part.

We were within minutes of their location and answered the call. An Army tractor-trailer, they were called low boys, loaded with boxed howitzer rounds, ran off the road and overturned in a rice paddy. Four soldiers rode on top of the shells when it flipped. Unfortunately, they were trapped under the load and were underwater.

When we arrived, another chopper was already there. I assume that they were the ones that made the distress call. They briefed us quickly, and we began working, trying to help get one of the guys pulled from under the rails on the side of the low boy. He was partially underwater, but the weight was causing the low boy to sink lower every minute we tried to pull him out. We could barely see through the muddy water, but it was obvious what we needed to do.

The only tools we had to free him were entrenching tools. (Small folding shovels that soldiers carry) We tried to use entrenching tools like axes and chop through the wooden rails to free the soldier. An entrenching tool could be folded in half to make it smaller, folded halfway down to make it more like a hoe, or fully extended to make it a shovel.

The other chopper crew found out that there were three soldiers in the cab and four riding on top of the howitzer shells on the low boy. Low boy? Picture a very long trailer with three or four-foot-high stake sides running around the outer edges to hold in cargo. This low boy was stacked to the top of the rails with long, narrow wooden boxes of ready-to-fire howitzer shells. Each of these shells and their wooden crate would have weighed more or less fifty pounds. My guess on the size of the low boy was that it would have been plus or minus forty feet long and eight feet wide. Adding the four feet height of the railing would give you somewhere around 800 or 900 shells. That's just a guess on my part, but I bet I am close. If that sounds like too many, let's just say there could have been 500 shells at 50 pounds each. That would have been 12 or 13 tons they were carrying, including the boxes.

After talking to the three soldiers in the cab, the first chopper crew learned that all seven were "stoned." We didn't have time to ask what they were stoned on. But, for the record, most guys in Vietnam smoked weed to get high. Some graduated to heroin, and a few even chewed betel nuts. Most used their drugs back at base camp, not in the field. Getting stoned and trying to avoid the enemy would have been stupid. These guys were stupid.

Three of the four riding on the low boy were still trapped under the shells, including the one we were trying to free. The fourth man had been thrown clear and needed medical attention but would survive. Unfortunately, no one had been able to find the other two, and it was assumed that they were crushed below the low boy and dead.

The one that was still alive and fighting to free himself, with our help, was trapped from his chest down. He was trapped under the load and the rails of the low boy. When we arrived, he was fighting to keep his head above water. He was fighting to get free but was pulled deeper into the water minute by minute. Two guys had him by his arms, trying to pull him free, but there was just too much weight holding him down. Plus, the low boy rails were centered between his ribs and pelvis, holding him in place, making it even more difficult to free him.

Then, a guy came running up with an entrenching tool and started trying to use it like an ax. He was trying to chop through the wood railing and free him. The guy's head was now below water, and he had stopped fighting to free himself.

When we could finally free him and pull him out, he had been underwater for maybe three or four minutes. The Crew Chief and Gunner immediately carried him to the chopper and started trying to revive him. He was still alive, but barely.

He had blood oozing from his ears and eyes. Bubbles and blood were coming from his nose and mouth. I remember seeing bubbles coming from one of his eyes. Maybe they were wiped from his nose and mouth while the Gunner was trying to give him mouth-to-mouth resuscitation. I don't know. Honestly, I couldn't tell for sure where they were coming from.

We were now in the air and flying toward Qui Nhon. We were trying to get this guy back for the medical attention that he needed. I looked back to see how he was doing and saw him looking at me. His eyes were open wide, and they were filled with fear. Then, at that very moment, the sorry son of a bitch locked eyes with mine. I could see in his eyes that he was pleading for me to help, and then they went blank.

The stupid son of a bitch had pulled me into his sorry-ass world and died while I looked at him. I couldn't help him. I couldn't do any more than I had to save him. Part of me died with him. I couldn't help him or myself. This wouldn't be the last time that I saw his face looking at me. He has visited me in my dreams many times over the years. He still does.

Why did I tell this story? For me, it was one of those pivotal moments in time when everything came into focus. A moment of clarity. I had just witnessed the senseless deaths of three teenagers. They were kids trapped in a war that they were too young and too immature to understand. Seven teenage soldiers were driving a semi on an elevated dirt roadway in a hostile country, a war zone. Unfortunately, they chose to get high while they were doing it. Senseless deaths in a senseless war.

Why did I tell you this story? You figure it out. It's for you to decide. Like I said before, whatever answer you come up with will be okay with me. As for me, I have revisited that night and seen that boy's face a thousand times since that day. I've seen the look in his eyes more times than I want to. But, no matter how much I want to, it's one of those things that I can't forget: that and a dozen more just like it.

Chapter 18:
I'm Going to be a Diamond Someday

Things were starting to get hot around LZ English. Just south of us, LZ Uplift was taking fire from the surrounding mountains almost every night. Every night LZ Uplift had incoming rounds, and they requested choppers to fly flare missions.

Flares were dropped to help see any large troop movements trying to break through the perimeter surrounding LZ Uplift.

Two nights later, one of my tent mates, whose tent was next to mine, was called on to fly a flare mission.

I also knew one of the crew members on the chopper, a fellow Mormon, Specialist Green. We weren't close, but we knew each other because of the church.

The following day, we all heard about the crash. I am guessing that because I knew two crew members, I was asked to help sift through the remains at the crash site.

*********Online information follows***********

Online you can find the following two reports on that flight. There are probably more, but these are the two that I will quote. One of them was written by me.

The official report reads as follows:

Information on U.S. Army helicopter UH-1D tail number 66-16330.
The Army purchased this helicopter 0467.
Total flight hours at this point 00000340.
Date 03/10/1968.
Incident number: 680310011ACD Accident Case Number
680310011 Total loss or fatality Accident.
Unit 61 AHC
The station for this helicopter was Phu Cat in South Vietnam.
UTM grid coordinates: BR914743
Number killed in accident + 4 . . Injured = 0 . .
Passengers = 0 costing 514554.
Original source(s) and document(s) from which the incident was created or updated: Defense Intelligence

Agency. Helicopter Loss database. Army Aviation Safety Center database. Also: OPERA (Operations Report.)
Loss to Inventory
Crew Members:
AC WO1 WIEBURG WILLIAM WARREN KIA
P WO1 SMITH STANLEY BRUCE KIA
CE SP4 HERDEBU DAN LEON KIA
G SP4 GREEN MICHAEL FRANK KIA

Accident Summary:
Shortly after takeoff, the aircraft was seen making a descending right turn. The aircraft crashed and burned, killing all occupants.

(End of report as shown online.)

Listed right below that report, I found one I added later, and I quote:

"War Story:
The crew was called out late one night for a flight to LZ Uplift. They, LZ Uplift, were taking sniper fire from the mountainside and had requested a flare mission flight. The Pilot reported the weather as a factor in declining the mission after arriving. He was then "ordered" to make the flight, an order he could have but did not refuse, as it was his choice. The chopper was then loaded with 51 flares. On taking off, the Huey hooked a skid on concertina wire and rolled into the ground, exploded, and burned. The additional heat from the 51 flares burning left little more than ashes of the aircraft. That morning, I and

several others were asked to sift through the ashes to try to locate any remains. While doing that, I picked up a piece of charcoal about 18 inches long and maybe 12 inches wide that weighed maybe a pound?? I could see a metallic piece embedded in the mass. Later, it was determined to be dog tags in the torso I had found. Ben Speed, former 61 AHC Pilot, Vietnam 1968."

Here is the deal. I don't remember making this report at the time or later. It sounds like something I would have said, but it sounds like it was edited. Most of what I remember is there, so I could have written it. I'm just not sure exactly when. It might have been an incident report that I was asked to make at the time, but I doubt that. There was a little more editorializing than I would have been able to do in an incident report.

On the other hand, it could have been something I wrote sometime after leaving Vietnam. It varies only a little from what I wrote in my Stressor Letter when I was asked to tell the VA what I thought caused my PTSD. So this could have been one of those stories.

More on this later.

****

There is no need to repeat what you can read online. I was told later that the charcoal brick I found, with the dog tags embedded, was my Mormon friend.

Chapter 19: Sweet Home Alabama (Lurp Story #2)

It was day two, and we had drawn the short straw. When the Lurps climbed aboard, we understood. We were the insertion team. Introductions were made, but one guy stood out more than the others. Mostly because I thought he was nuts. No, not nuts. Bat shit crazy. He was due to rotate out of the country and back to Alabama in less than a week. Six days. He would probably spend the next five days in the field, come back in, pack, and leave the country that day if he was lucky. If he stayed out six days, he would have even less time, if he made it at all.

They offered him a pass on this mission, and he didn't take it. He was determined to get in one last mission. This guy loved what he did. I wish I could remember his name. I remember his buddies called him "Alabama."

Alabama was laughing and seemed genuinely happy to go on one more mission with his buddies. One minute, he was talking about his home in Alabama and how much he wanted to go home, and the next minute, he was talking about the mission and what they would do. He was a gung-ho SOB, or maybe he just had a bad case of nerves and excitement. Who knows? Some guys get silly when they are trying to calm themselves. I don't think that was the case here.

I think he was genuinely excited about going on this mission.

The insertion was a textbook operation. No complications. Now, it was time to wait. Put them in, take them out. If all went well, I had four, maybe five days of milk runs coming my way.

After returning from Firebase Meade and safely delivering Father Murphy, we expected another late afternoon milk run. But that's not what happened.

Our Lurps had been discovered. They needed immediate extraction. They were being chased, and they were taking heavy fire. Worse yet, they had been found by a large NVA unit. These weren't VC gorillas; they were the disciplined, well-trained, and well-equipped Regular Army troops chasing my Lurps. Alabama and his team needed a ride back to the base.

There wasn't time to prepare. We needed to fuel up and leave as soon as possible. That meant that there would be just two choppers. Ours and the Command and Control ship from yesterday. Maybe not even the same commander on board the C and C. No gunships. No help. No time to arrange anything more than going back to where we dropped them off and trying to make contact on the radio. Once we made radio contact, they could talk us in.

Great plans usually fall short of our expectations anyway. This was flying by the seat of your pants. "Just get in, pick them up, and get them out as fast as you can," were our orders. The only good thing about this mission was the weather. It was good.

Mountain weather was always unpredictable. Today's weather was great. No stiff winds, no clouds. It was hot, but it was always hot in the summer in Vietnam, even in the mountains. These weren't fourteeners. They were oners mostly, with maybe a few one-and-a-halfers.

When we arrived, the Lurps were already in contact with the Command and Control chopper. They were trying to direct one of us in by the sound of our helicopters. The problem was that the NVAs were close enough to hear the radio chatter, and they were doing a better job finding the Lurps than we were.

Now, the Lurps were whispering more than talking on their radio. You could tell that they were running. They had to catch their breath every time they tried to speak. Whispering isn't an option when you are out of breath.

Their instructions to us were to stop calling. The radio gave away their position every time they stopped and found cover. But that probably didn't matter right then. They were still running. Their location was changing by the minute, and they couldn't stop and wait for us to pick them up, even if we found them. Now, they were taking fire from two different directions. One side was close enough that they could hear them reloading. Shots from behind were getting closer.

Simply put, there was no point in them trying to talk now. They couldn't tell us where they were. They didn't have any idea. No one had time to look at a map anyway. Now, they were just trying to follow the sound of our chopper. Their last message was for us to find an extraction point, and they would come to us. Go a little farther up the valley than we are now and wait. They would come to us.

Our plan was to get as close to them as we could safely and then guide them toward a point where we could sit down long enough to pick them up. That's how screwed up the situation was. We were trying to tell them where we would pick them up. Instead, they were telling us not to use the radio.

In their next radio contact, they told us they were receiving fire from three sides. As a result, they could only go in one direction. Their fear was that they were being forced into an ambush. They needed to be extracted now, or it would be too late.

There wasn't a need for radio silence now. The NVA could see the Lurps, and they were shooting at them. The Lurps could see the NVA. They could no longer outrun the NVA. They were reaching the end of what was turning out to be a box canyon. We were right above them now and taking fire ourselves.

There was an opening in the trees just ahead of their position. It was large enough for us to land, but just barely. So when we saw them running through the trees toward the clearing, we started trying to land just before them.

We could see them running into the clearing when we touched down. Next, I saw an NVA soldier lying in a prone position on a large boulder just ahead of where we had landed. Maybe 200 yards, maybe less. He was firing a machine gun mounted on a folding tripod. I could see his face, but not much more. I couldn't understand why he wasn't hitting us. Then I realized he was firing at the Lurps as they were running toward the chopper, and two of the Lurps were firing at him.

I looked around at the Lurps again. They were coming toward us, and I was trying to judge how long before they would jump aboard. I could see all of them running. One jumped in, and a second, then a third. I looked back just in time to see Alabama running forward and then flying back. He fell and didn't move. A fourth man jumped in, and the fifth and last man was on board.

We started pulling up. One of the Lurps grabbed his leg. He had just taken a small-caliber round from below. I could still hear firing as we cleared the trees, but it was behind us. They were probably firing at the sound of the chopper. They couldn't see us through the trees now.

One of the Lurps, a black guy, was holding his ear. His ear lobe was bleeding, and a small part of his ear was missing. One of the other Lurps was working on the guy who was shot in the leg. He was trying to stop the bleeding.

I remember pulling pitch while we were trying to take off. I remember someone saying that I was over-torquing the chopper. I remember looking out and seeing the soldier on the rock below still shooting at us. I looked over at Alabama and saw NVA soldiers standing over his body. I remember feeling the other pilot taking the controls. Then, I remember everything going black. Maybe 3 or 4 seconds passed, maybe more. I don't know. I was out. This was the first time, but it would not be the last.

We made it, minus Alabama. We saved five of the six men, and I felt like crap. Then I saw the black guy looking at the blood on his arm. He had been hit in his arm and ear. He didn't say anything. He just sat looking at his arm. Then, finally, he started tearing his shirt sleeve back and trying to see how bad he was hit. The guy with the leg wound said, "It was a clean shot. In and out. No bone." He was squatting down and looked like he was about to fall over. The other three hadn't been hit. They were fine. They looked tired and like a group of guys that had just had the crap scared out of them. Other than that, they would live to fight another day. The chopper took a couple more rounds while pulling out of the pickup area, but nothing critical was hit. We were flying back to the base.

Late that afternoon, one of the Lurps came to my tent and tried to give me something for pulling them out.

He wanted to thank me. Why me? Why not the rest of the crew? I didn't understand. Maybe he had already seen the rest of the crew. He handed me a little white box, and as he handed it to me, he slid it open. Laying on white cotton was a finger.

It looked like it had been boxed in a jewelry store. White box. Snow white cotton. Sliding cover. I didn't know what to say. I just stood there. I'm guessing that he understood, and he closed the box and said he would be right back, and he left. Ten minutes later, he returned, but this time, he handed me a pistol that he had taken off a dead NVA officer. It was a Star. It looked like a German Luger. I acted appropriately pleased and thanked him for it.

It's a little early for me to bring this up, but that pistol had a story of its own later.

Later that evening, I went to one of my flight leaders, a Captain, and asked if I could talk with him. I told him about blacking out and asked if he thought I should see the flight surgeon. He seemed genuinely concerned, but not for my safety. He kept telling me that I should be careful. I might get grounded. I tried to explain that I was more worried about the safety of my passengers than myself. "For God's sake, I blacked out at the controls."

Today, thinking about that talk, I think maybe part of what I said was a lie. It did scare the crap out of me. I was worried about killing others, but I had to be concerned about killing myself.

After a few minutes, my Captain's final advice was to wait a few days and see if it happened again. Wait until after I have some time to recover from today's flight. Then came the warning. "The 10th Combat Aviation Battalion Commander doesn't like it when it has a pilot that doesn't want to fly. Be careful, Lieutenant." I understood his warning. He was telling me to suck it up, keep flying, and hope it didn't happen again. I knew it was stupid advice, but I knew better than to argue about it there. I remembered those classes in flight school.

It happened several more times after that. There were lots of those short periods when I blacked out for four or five seconds and then went back to normal. To say that it only happened when I was frightened would be putting too broad of a brush on it. It happened when I was under stress, which was an everyday thing. It was part of what I did for a living and was one reason I loved flying. I loved pushing it to the limit and feeling that surge of adrenaline flowing through my system. I loved the rush that came with it. For those few seconds, I was alive.

I know how that sounds, but that's how it was. Ask any combat veteran, and he will tell you that they became addicted to the adrenalin rushes. It was something that I couldn't figure out, and if I couldn't figure out what was going on, I couldn't fix it. Was it because I was afraid? Screw you! I looked at what I had done to save those five guys. Yes, I lost one of them, but the other five were alive because I sat there... we sat there. We sat perfectly still while looking out that windscreen, knowing that little shit on that boulder was spraying our chopper with a machine gun. We sat there longer than we should have, waiting for those guys to jump in. I wasn't a damn coward. I wasn't trying to find cover. I sat there and watched rounds flying past. Something else was happening, and I needed help figuring out what it was.

The next morning, the Lurps formed a search team and returned to recover Alabama's body. It took them two more days to find him. The NVA had placed his body on a large boulder in an open spot among the trees. We speculated that they wanted us to be able to see him from the air. It might have been a trap for us. It could have been a warning. We didn't know. Maybe they were showing respect. Perhaps they put it in the hot sun so that we could find it.

It did make it more difficult for the Lurps to find the body. As for me, I think that they wanted to place it where it would be seen by choppers flying over. They knew that we would come back for the body. We were like them when it came to removing our dead. We did, and they did, whenever it was possible. "No man left behind." It was a moral problem, leaving dead and wounded behind.

Warning: skip this next paragraph if you have a weak stomach.

Alabama's body had been left on top of a boulder in direct sunlight for two and a half days. He had started to decay. To put it bluntly, he stunk. The Lurps put Alabama in a body bag so that we could fly in, sit down next to it, put him in the cargo area quickly, and fly out without becoming a target.

It was a good plan, but it couldn't be done. The smell was overpowering. We were ashamed that we couldn't do it with greater respect, but, in the end, the Lurps wrapped his body in rope and left fifty feet for us to tie on to so that the body would remain outside the chopper far enough that we couldn't smell him. Lord, forgive me. We flew his body back to Qui Nhon with their homemade sling.

(Don't read this next paragraph if you are easily upset by gruesome details.)

There was more than another problem putting Alabama in the chopper with our passengers. The Lurps thought that it was demoralizing. The NVA had cut Alabama's testicles off and placed them in his mouth. His eyes looked like they had been pushed in with a knife or stick. It appeared that they dragged him to where they had left his body. His arms and legs had been pulled out of their sockets. His body lay in a most disturbing position. His wounds were infested with all manner of insects and what I think were maggots. Dragging him as far as they did damage the body even more. Even without the odor, seeing a human body as mutilated as this one was difficult. It was our fault, I guess. We wouldn't have seen him if we had waited until they placed Alabama into the body bag we had brought.

Before you get all judgmental, I should warn you that our boys did some shitty things to the NVA and VC. Remember that finger he offered me. He was wearing a necklace made from a string of human ears around his neck when he showed me his gift. Leaving an ace of spades in their mouths was common. It wasn't a nice war. It was a war. Vietnamese people believed they would go wherever they went when they died, just as they left. Taking an ear or finger would be a constant reminder of the war for all eternity. We did it, and they did it. It was meant to work on an army's morale. It worked on mine. There were a lot of us that hated it, but it was what it was.

My Crew Chief and Gunner spent the rest of the afternoon trying to remove the odor from the cargo area where they had first placed the body. Unfortunately, the few minutes that Alabama's body was in our chopper caused an odor that lingered for weeks. Constantly reminding us of what we saw that day.

Chapter 20: High Blood Pressure

After flying multiple new missions, I was finally allowed to see the flight surgeon. The long-awaited appointment had been granted. I was back in Qui Nhon and sitting in the infirmary waiting to be seen by the doctor. I could finally talk with someone about the blackouts and my concerns that I might kill everyone on board, myself included, if I had one at the wrong time. Wrong time? It wasn't lost on me that there was no good time to blackout in flight.

After an hour-long physical, the verdict was in. I had high blood pressure, and it was high enough that the doctor grounded me for three days. It was required by regulations. After three days, they would check my blood pressure again.

The doctor explained that I had three days to figure out a way to get my blood pressure down. He also explained that, as a pilot, he could not lower my blood pressure with drugs or prescriptions. I couldn't take blood pressure medicine to bring it down and still fly. Next, he sent me back to my unit and grounded me until our next visit. I was put on light duty for three days.

That afternoon, the Commander called me into his office and informed me that I was under house arrest. I would be confined to quarters except for meals at the officer's mess. He told me that I was being charged with malingering.

In a war zone, malingering was a serious charge with severe penalties. Not the least of which would be time in Fort Leavenworth. The Colonel had a little smirk on his face while explaining in detail how he was going to make an example of me. How I would be the first and the last one to attempt to avoid flying this way. I was tempted to ask him what he thought I was trying to do? But I knew better. I kept my mouth shut.

He had two MPs (Military Policemen) escort me back to the BOQ (Bachelor Officer Quarters) and stand guard outside my door. Where would I go? I was escorted back to the flight surgeon's office three days later, and he confirmed his diagnosis. I had high blood pressure, and I was grounded permanently unless God himself chose to lower my blood pressure.

Let's review this again. I want the world to know exactly what I was being charged for. I was blacking out during flight, and I worried about it. The flight surgeon grounded me for three days until he could recheck my blood pressure after I rested. Three days later, when he checked my blood pressure, he grounded me permanently. What was I attempting to do? What exactly was malingering? How does one give himself high blood pressure so that he can malinger? I felt like I was missing something.

This time, when they sent me back to the BOQ, it was without an escort. The thought occurred to me that this Colonel was mad (not angry mad, mad as in nuts) enough that he might want me to try to escape just so that he could shoot me himself. I thought about it for a minute and then laughed. I walked back to the BOQ, sat down on my bunk, and tried to figure out what was happening. What in God's name had I done wrong? No one was looking at the missions that I had flown. The risks that I had taken to save lives while risking my own. It wasn't lost on me that this Colonel was doing this to make a point for the rest of his pilots. It sure as hell wasn't lost on me that I was being made an example of.

The next day, I had a visitor. He told me he was an attorney from the JAG and was there to represent me at my Court Martial. Somehow, this didn't make me feel warm and fuzzy all over. So far, every officer I had talked to was trying to send me to prison.

We talked for a few minutes. He asked me to tell him my side of the story, and I did my best. He looked confused and asked me if I had refused to fly in combat? I said that I had not. In fact, I had flown several missions after asking to see the flight surgeon. He stood up and told me that I shouldn't worry. This wouldn't take long, and he left.

The following morning, he returned and told me that the court-martial would hear his arguments today and that I would not be required to attend. But I should remain in my quarters until he returned.

Several hours later, he returned and said everything went well and that the court would meet later that day and decide what actions they would take. Actions they would take? What actions? The good news was that I was no longer confined to my quarters. I could go to the officer's club if I wished.

Nature has a way of knowing when we need a big hug. She knows when we need a pat on the back. Today was not that day. My mail finally caught up with me, and I had one letter. It was from my wife. She was asking me for a divorce. So maybe it was time for me to go to the officer's club and drink a few.

I sat in the bar, drinking my gin and tonics. I had missed at least four or five days. I was behind, and I wasn't going to take that damned quinine pill again. After my second or third drink and thinking about my life in general, I began to think about my wife and children and how much I loved them. I realized for the first time that I could go to prison for having high blood pressure and never see them again.

Maybe it was the gin and tonic, or maybe it was just me, but I was tired. I felt defeated. I leaned forward on the bar and asked the Vietnamese bartender if he had any APCs. (All Purpose Capsules. The military's answer to Tylenol and aspirin.) He handed me a full bottle, and I poured out and counted fifty pills. I asked for a glass of water and swallowed them all, one handful at a time. I got up and walked back to the BOQ.

For the first time in a long time, I felt some measure of relief. I was tired, and I was sleepy. I lay down and went to sleep, believing I would never have to go through another day like this one again. It felt good. I fell asleep almost immediately.

I woke up the following day with a screaming headache. My ears were ringing so loud I couldn't think. My stomach hurt. When I threw up, I decided that I needed to go on sick call one more time.

When the medics finished with me, they sent me down the hall to the psychiatrist. Long story short, when we were behind closed doors, he asked me if I planned to do it again. I said no, I did not. He reached over, touched my wedding band, and asked if I loved my family. I told him that I did. I meant it.

When I tried to tell him about last night's revelation, he asked me why I chose APCs to do what I did? "Did you actually think that they would kill you?" I didn't think it could get any worse, but I was wrong. Now, I not only felt like hell physically, but I felt stupid to boot.

By now, I guessed that everyone on the base knew what I had done. I went back to my room and waited. Then I started wondering, what, precisely, does one take for a headache you get from taking too many aspirins?

My thoughts were soon interrupted when my attorney stopped in and told me that it was over. I was going to be reassigned to Battalion Headquarters in Dong Ba Thin later that week. Then he said that the Colonel's actions were being questioned and that he would not be allowed to talk to me again. No further actions against me would be taken.

So far as I know, nothing about that day or my visit with the psychiatrist was ever added to my medical file. My life was about to turn in a completely different direction. It was over. I had survived. No one ever said anything about my sick call visit. I don't think they ever found out what I had done. If they did, they probably thought they knew why.

I sat down and wrote my wife that night, asking her to reconsider. Actually, I don't remember exactly what I asked her. We did try and work it out later when I returned home.

When I got to Dong Ba Thin, one more action was taken. They held a board meeting to determine what to do with me. The only question they asked me was, would I be interested in flying "Bird-dogs"? Bird dogs were single-winged, single-engine, small, fixed-wing airplanes that the Army used primarily as artillery spotters.

I wasn't quite sure if they knew that the flight surgeon would have to clear me to fly bird dogs or any other aircraft. I still would have to meet the same physical requirements that I had to meet as a chopper pilot. I don't think that they knew everything that happened in Qui Nhon. I told them no, I wasn't interested in learning to fly fixed-wing aircraft.

The following day, I was assigned to the 10th Combat Aviation Battalion in Dong Ba Thin as the assistant battalion signal officer. I would work under Capt. Pilgrim. I always liked that name. I liked him as well.

He was a good man. But he was not an adventurous man like most chopper pilots. He didn't like risk-taking. In fact, he was the best I have ever seen at looking the other way. He was a career man.

By the end of their first tour, most helicopter pilots looked forward to going home as a civilian. Not all of us, but most of us didn't want to fly in Vietnam for the rest of our lives. No matter what you have heard, we weren't all adrenaline junkies. We all loved flying, but most of us loved living too.

I don't think Capt. Pilgram had a clue what he would do with me, but I helped him figure that out a few days later. I had a natural talent that even I didn't realize I had.

When my Southern upbringing came into play, I could talk you into anything, or more to the point, I could talk you out of anything. I was a natural-born scrounger. I was soon as good at scrounging as I was as a chopper pilot. I was a damned good pilot. I was a cowboy at heart, and that was how I flew.

Chapter 21: Korean Discipline

This might be the shortest chapter in this book. While I was back at Lane, waiting to find out what would happen to me. I met and became friends with a

Korean Officer, Lieutenant Kim. Our friendship was little more than a meeting at the Officer's Club twice a week and having a meal and/or drinks together. I enjoyed his company, and he seemed to enjoy mine.

Our routine was such that we met two days a week. I don't remember which two days. It was a long time ago. We didn't plan anything other than being there on time. We just met and shared our thoughts and had a meal and maybe a few drinks.

One evening, Lt. Kim's driver met me on my way to the Officer's Club. He apologized for Lt. Kim and said that he wasn't feeling well that evening and would not be able to meet with me.

I could see that Kim's driver was hiding something, so I pressed and asked why he wasn't meeting me. His driver's answer surprised me. I knew that the Korean soldiers were "take no prisoners" hardcore soldiers, but this was an extreme that I didn't know existed.

The night before, Lt. Kim was the Officer of the Day. The Koreans provided our base perimeter security. Kim found one of his guards asleep on duty. The following day, during the formation, Kim called out the guard's NCO, stood him at attention in front of the formation, and then proceeded to beat the hell out of him. I suppose for not knowing that one of his men was sleeping on guard duty. The Sergeant took his beating, standing up each time he was knocked down, and took his next beating. When the Sergeant could no longer stand back up, Kim walked over to the soldier, pulled out his pistol, and shot him in the face.

I asked the driver if this was normal, and he said it was for soldiers who fell asleep guarding our base. Then, I asked what would happen to the Korean soldier's body. Kim's driver pointed to the crematorium. He said that the soldier's body had already been cremated and his ashes thrown in the trash.

I knew the Koreans cremated their soldiers when they were killed in battle and sent the ashes back to their families. This guy's ashes went into the trash.

Chapter 22: Natural Born Scrounger

The 10th CAB, Combat Aviation Battalion, arrived in Vietnam and was declared operational on the 20th of November 1967. They were at the hub of this new concept. They had assault helicopter companies, a medivac company, an avionics unit, and a maintenance company. All were under the control of the 10th CAB.

As the scope of their operations grew and developed, they were becoming more and more out of touch with the needs of each specific unit.

They discovered they needed more and different equipment than was first assigned. Getting some of these things was not easy.

That's where I came in. I didn't mind arranging trades or just appropriating things needed more by one of my units than by its current owner. People were risking their lives to accomplish their missions and sometimes risking their lives unnecessarily because they didn't have what they needed to achieve that mission. So, I didn't see a moral issue with my system. We all worked for the same people. The Army, Navy, Marines, and the Air Force... especially the Air Force, had all been given equipment to accomplish their missions. Some were given more than needed, some less. The Air Force had more. We had less.

I probably should explain my thinking back then. The Army and the Marines were combat ground pounders by nature. Helicopter pilots were there to move the ground-pounders around more efficiently and to keep them supplied with ammo and food.

They each needed the tools of their trade. The Air Force performed a critical mission, no doubt. But their ground combat needs were "just in case" needs. I didn't feel that their need for specific equipment was at the same level as the needs of the Marines and Army. At least, that's how I felt at the time. I could have been just a little one-sided, maybe. But, if we were at an Army vs. Air Force football game, I would be sitting on the Army's side of the field. So, yes, I was prejudiced.

Cam Ranh Bay Air Force base was a short 45-minute drive from Dong Ba Thin Annex. Cam Ranh was one of Vietnam's largest and safest seaports. Almost everything we received came through Cam Ranh.

When President Johnson came to Vietnam, he landed at Cam Ranh Bay. So why would they need all those combat supplies?

I felt obligated to help the war effort in any way I could. Even if it meant personal sacrifices. Remember that pistol that the Lurp gave me?

One of the companies assigned to the 10th CAB was high up in the mountains and more than an hour's flight from Dong Ba Thin. Its real estate had been cut out of the middle of the jungle. It was on the edge of a vast rubber tree plantation. Its location was so unsafe there that it had more "buildings" underground than above ground.

To get to this outpost, you had to fly through a high mountain pass, usually cloud-covered, especially in the early mornings and always in the evenings. This made it dangerous for pilots to return to their company, especially late every evening and at night.

Flying out was somewhat safer. You could always turn back and return to base if the pass was cloud covered... Unless the mission's priority was higher than the risk to the pilots, That was always a possibility.

The underground buildings were not so much bunkers as they were workspaces. That company was mortared so often that it was easier to bury the Conex containers they worked out of and keep everything in one piece. The additional benefit was obvious. They were cooler. People were safer in those first moments when the mortars started coming in... before anyone could make it to cover. The above-ground buildings were being destroyed faster than they could rebuild them, so they moved underground. And yes, they slept underground, also.

The fact that this camp was surrounded by high ground and mountains, a rubber tree plantation, and was in the lowest spot in the area made it the ideal target of frequent and brutal mortar attacks.

The problem that this created for the 10th CAB was that every time this unit was attacked, the 10th CAB went on high alert. The next problem this created was we couldn't reach this unit at night by radio. The radios issued to this unit didn't work as well that high up at night. We needed to be able to respond if required, and we couldn't do that until the following morning. That meant that we had to stay on alert until the threat was over. We had no way of knowing when it was over until we could reach them by radio... which we couldn't do at night when most of these mortar attacks took place. In fact, they were coming under attack sometimes, as often as twice a week.

The recent Tet Offensive had not been as effective as the NVA hoped it would be, but it was not over, especially up in this remote mountain base. The NVA considered the Tet Offensive as the beginning of their great offensive. It was not over. It had only just begun.

Small talk in the Battalion Signal office centered around how much new high-frequency radios were needed. I overheard Capt. Pilgrim talking about these radios, their benefits, and how badly they were needed there.

All of this created several problems for the 10th CAB. The obvious problem was that everyone went on alert when that company in the mountains came under attack. If we lost radio contact, we had to remain on alert until the situation was resolved. No one knew when this happened without radio contact. This would often require the Colonel to stay in the TOC, Tactical Operations Center, sometimes all night.

Worse yet, not all these attacks started during the day. Some didn't start until late at night when they couldn't reach the 10th CAB. So there were times when the Battalion should have been on alert but had no way of knowing it. This created several problems. How would we know when to send help if we weren't aware they were in trouble?

Then I heard the silly talk start. "What if they had a non-directional beacon to help the pilots fly through the pass when it was cloud covered." There had been several helicopters lost due to "cumulus-graniteus." (Clouds with rocks in them.) It was a common problem for Pilots in Vietnam. Especially when they had to fly at night, in bad weather, and in the mountains.

I personally experienced a close call flying over Uplift Pass. It was cloudy, and we couldn't see where we were, so we decided to turn on our searchlight. We were lucky. We turned them on just in time to see that we were about to fly into the side of the mountain. It scared the crap out of us. Why were we flying with our searchlights off that night? We were getting shot at. Uplift pass had NVA all over it.

Here is where I realized my mission as the Assistant Battalion Signal Officer at the 10th Combat Aviation Battalion. I discovered that there were plenty of these radios at Cam Ranh AFB. They had warehouses full of equipment that they weren't using. Equipment that would save the lives of our troops was sitting in their warehouse unused. I saw that as a potential win-win situation.

As luck would have it, it was my turn to be paymaster this month, which meant I had the duty of guarding and delivering everyone's pay in cash. This included that outpost up in the mountains. I was going to see firsthand what their situation was.

Going there was an eye-opener. After seeing how they lived and listening to their close calls firsthand, I couldn't just sit and watch. I knew what I was going to do. I had a plan. Down South in the States, I learned early that solutions could easily be reached when you came begging with a gift in your hand instead of a hat.

Chapter 23: Officer's Club Mishap

Our Officer's Club was a well-run, well-stocked entertainment center, and we had one of the best club managers in the Army running it, and I knew his weakness. He was one of those fellows who looked at the war through the bottom of a beer mug. We were getting all the "glory" while he had to work in a beer hall. I wasn't there to change his attitude. No matter how many holes I saw in his argument, I was there to take advantage of it.

I had my Astra Star Model A, Luger twin, cleaned and oiled. It was going to be my bait. That following day, I walked over to the officer's club with my pistol in hand. Chief Warrant Officer Jones or Smith, use any name you are comfortable with, was there cleaning up and restocking the bar all alone. He was excited to see me and the pistol I had previously told him about.

I asked him if he knew anyone who might be interested in it. I just didn't need it any longer. Too many bad memories, I said. I knew that he was hooked. "How much do you want for it? Where did you get it? Where did the LRRP get it?" His questions were too specific to be thinking of someone for me to sell it to. He wanted it himself, and I knew it. I had him right where I needed him to be.

Then, a funny thing happened. Not funny, Ha-Ha, but funny odd. He asked me if he could hold it. "Sure," I said, handing it to him with the clip filled with ammo. He immediately took the clip, shoved it into the pistol, and jacked the slide.

It fired. He did not pull the trigger. It simply fired.

Here's the odd part. He did it again, and it fired a second time, blowing a second hole in his office wall. Now, sirens were sounding everywhere. Mr. Jones took my pistol, re-wrapped it in the rag I brought, and locked it in his safe. Then, we both walked out to face our demise.

There wasn't anyone waiting to arrest us. Instead, people were running up and down the streets and out of buildings, and they were all armed. When we asked one of them what was going on, he said, "We are under attack. A sniper shot two rounds into the Red Cross Donut Dollies' trailer." He when on to say that no one had been hit, but it scared the crap out of the ladies. We could do nothing sensible at this point except go back into the officer's club and wait for the excitement to end.

Mr. Jones and I decided it would be best if we didn't mention his little mishap and forgot it ever happened. Then he did what I expected he would do. He asked me what I wanted for the pistol. He was still interested. I said a case of Johnnie Walker Black Label. Without missing a beat, he offered his hand, and the deal was sealed on the spot.

Note: That model Astra Star 9 mm had a slide that fits equally well right side up or upside down. If you put it upside down, the firing pin would strike the cartridge when you loaded it and cause it to fire. By the way, I was told I was mistaken and that there was no such pistol as an Astra Star model A pistol. There was. It was a limited edition made during WW2, I think. I'm not sure about that part. It was created to help fill the need for more Lugers. Later, they were sold off to other countries. They were made, and I owned one for a short time.

Back to the story.

After several hours, the alert was called off. Extra guards were placed on our perimeter and at the Donut Dollies' trailer. The officer's club was allowed to re-open, and burgers and beer were sold at a record pace. No one was ever any the wiser.

I would like to apologize to one of the Red Cross ladies. Miss Jodie Rouse. I'm sorry for any discomfort this event caused you. I'm sure you understand why Mr. Jones and I didn't apologize at the time. You were my salvation that year, and I would have never done anything to harm you.

Chapter 24: The Big Trade

The next day, I told Capt. Pilgrim that I needed a couple guys and the use of two vehicles, one jeep and one deuce and a half. I explained that I was going to do some scrounging at Cam Ranh. He smiled and said he didn't want to know any details. I would be on my own. Then he asked me why I needed a two-and-a-half-ton truck?

"What was I going after?" "Radios," I said. "just radios." He looked at me and said, "Radios? We need some radios." He started making a list. Then he said that one of our guys knew how to get to the right depot at Cam Ranh, and he would send him as one of my helpers. I assumed that was the good captain's way of saying yes. He handed me his list, and I added a non-directional beacon. Capt. Pilgrim smiled and started walking away, then stopped, looked back, and said loud enough that everyone heard him. "I don't think this is a good idea, Lieutenant." He smiled and softly said, "Good luck," and walked away. He had deniability. I was on my own.

We found the Avionics depot without any problems. The Specialist 4th class that Capt. Pilgrim sent with me knew how to get there, and he introduced me to the Air Force Sergeant in charge as soon as we arrived.

I immediately set out to win him over. I told him about our problems in the mountains and how troops were getting killed because they couldn't get in touch with each other. I told him about the never-ending alerts we were going through, and then I told him why I was there. We were losing good people. In the middle of this tale of woe, I motioned for my Spec.4 to go to the Jeep. He knew what I wanted. He knew why. He returned, carrying the box with Johnnie Walker stamped in large black letters on the side. All conversations ended. We handed the Air Force Sergeant one case of scotch whisky. He walked back into his office without saying a word. I could see him opening the box and pulling out a bottle. He opened it and then took a sip. Sealed it and put it back in the case and then walked back out into the loading area and asked if I had a list.

We had a deal.

We spent the next two- or three hours loading radios into our truck. When I saw that the sergeant's patients were starting to grow thin, I motioned for my guys to stop. I thanked the sergeant and asked if he had an old load receipt I could flash when we went through the gate. He said he did, picked out one, and handed it to me. I was ready to leave... but something was bothering me. I pointed to the large wooden crate that had Baldwin stamped on one end and asked the sergeant if that was what I thought it was? "Yes, it's a Baldwin grand piano. It's been sitting here in my way since I arrived back in 1967." Then he asked me if I wanted it?" He helped us load that one himself. He drove the forklift.

Note: I had several rules when it came to scrounging. I never violated these rules. I didn't want to end up in Leavenworth. Facing that possibility once was enough. One of those rules was that I only traded for things that benefited my troops, not me. I never traded for anything for myself. I wanted no personal gain of any kind.

I never took anything that would hurt those losing it. What rules the other guys lived by were none of my business. That was between them and their conscience. I did not steal anything. I traded. Some traders were better at their craft than others. I felt comfortable working with them all.

When we returned to the 10th CAB Headquarters, I talked with my Specialist 4th Class and his assistant. I told them to take the piano to the officer's club and unload it there. Tell Mr. Jones to keep it quiet, and I will explain later. Tell him not to let anyone know where he got the piano. He could take credit for finding it if he wanted. Then, I talked with my guys and explained what would happen if we got caught. I explained the penalty for stealing... scrounging equipment from the military. I scared the crap out of my helpers. Now, we were a team. I wasn't worried about one of them giving me up.

Next, we went to Capt. Pilgrim and asked where he wanted the radios and other equipment to go. My helpers offloaded everything and got back to work.

In the meantime, I went to the officer's club and arranged a trade for the piano. I only wanted two boxes of T-bone steaks and a box of lobster tails. If I remember correctly, these were 40-pound boxes. These were to be taken to the Headquarters and Headquarters Detachment of the 10th CAB and given to the Colonel for use that weekend at our cookout. I made sure that Mr. Jones knew not to give me credit for the steaks, lobster, or piano. Mr. Jones could take credit for all of it. In fact, I insisted.

More than a week had passed since I acquired the radios and the non-directional beacon. Capt. Pilgrim felt that the best place to hide them was to simply install them where they were needed and start using them. They were quickly installed, tested, and made ready to use. Now, all we needed to do was prove their worth.

More than a couple weeks passed before our little mountain company came under attack again and put us all on alert. The problem in the past had always been that we lost contact with the company at sundown, and we stayed on alert until the next day when we could contact them again. However, this time, things were different.

The Colonel jumped into his Jeep and told his driver to take him to the TOC. Someone, probably Capt. Pilgrim handed the Colonel one of the new high-frequency radio mics and said the company was "on the line." This caught the Colonel by surprise. He had never been able to talk to his people until he was in the Tactical Operations Center. Even then, only if it was still daylight. He was probably a little shocked or just surprised, but he was also curious and probably asked Capt. Pilgrim, too many questions.

That night, the alert was over one hour after the attack started, and the Colonel was able to return to his poker game. The same game that took place every night. I found out later that he spent most of the evening trying to find out who knew where those radios came from. I think that's why Capt. Pilgrim was in the Colonel's Jeep and showed him how to operate his new radio. Pilgrim didn't play poker, and I think he wanted to cover his ass before the next morning's staff meeting. I'm just guessing, but I would bet my soul on it. The next day, Capt. Pilgram couldn't look me in the eye when we talked. He was as guilty as sin, and I knew it. What's worse, he knew I knew. It was the end of a short friendship, at least for me.

Chapter 25: The Atta'boy Meeting

That morning after the staff meeting, the Colonel called me into his office along with most of his staff... except Capt. Pilgrim. He went over the events of the previous evening. Then he asked me if I knew anything about it. I knew it would be hopeless to lie and stupid to confess, so I said I had heard about it. Then he told me about the radios up in the mountains and the non-directional beacon. He knew about all of it. The more details he gave me, the more I knew that Capt. Pilgrim had sold me down the river.

What I didn't understand was whether the Colonel praising me or setting me up? He talked about how great it was to speak to his people from his jeep and later in the Tactical Op-Center, even after dark. How he could talk to his people any time he needed. He talked about how great it was that they could fly in and out of the camp through the pass, homing in on that new non-directional beacon, NDB. This went on for several minutes, and everyone had smiles on their faces until he stopped and said, "You do understand that I'm going to court-martial you, don't you?"

My stomach fell through my ass and landed on the floor below. Another court-martial? Then he smiled the biggest smile yet and said, "You have two options. You can become the new Battalion Supply Officer, sign the property books, and take responsibility for this new unauthorized equipment. Or I will be forced to court-martial you."

He said that I would have to account for all the property, not on those books. All those things that were not issued to our unit. He continued by saying, good intentions or not, he wasn't going to jail for me. He said as much. Then he pushed two large narrow ledgers in front of me and said, "You decide." I signed them both.

What I didn't know, and the Colonel hadn't told me, was that these two property books hadn't been signed for in more than 4 or 5 months. Half of the camp's people had either left or were newly arrived during that period. We were a headquarters company and not a combat unit. Most of the officers were here on a temporary basis. Many were here to get the time needed to maintain their flight status and keep getting flight pay. People were coming and leaving daily, and their weapons and equipment were coming and going with them. None of those changes had been recorded for more than six months. I checked, and more than half of the weapons in the armory did not match the serial numbers in our inventory. There were more weapons in stock than we had on the books. Two helicopters were missing. Two Choppers!

The previous supply officer had been granted compassionate leave to return to the States for a complicated childbirth that his wife might not survive. I'm guessing that it didn't go well. He did not return. He was permanently transferred to a stateside assignment without returning. That meant the property books had not been appropriately transferred when he left. No one would sign them after 5 or 6 months of neglect.

The following supply officer refused to sign the property books. He was transferred, and the next officer refused to sign them. To make matters worse, the supply sergeant had rotated back to the States, and the new guy didn't have a clue.

I was starting to understand the shit storm that I was in. Now I understood why the Colonel was smiling. He would have been responsible for what happened as much as anyone. Instead, he had just found his get-out-of-jail-free card. And it had my picture on it.

I did my best to find and account for all the missing weapons. I tried to find out who they were assigned to now and where they were? But without records, it was anyone's guess. I found most of the other missing equipment, but not all of it.

The two helicopters were easy to track down. One was a replacement for a chopper that was destroyed by enemy fire. I guessed that the other missing chopper was the totaled one after it was transferred back to the 10th. It had been either salvaged or cannibalized for parts. That accounted for the second missing chopper. That was the only solution that would account for the two missing helicopters. But I didn't have any way of proving it. There wasn't any paperwork to back up my theory.

Here's the worst part: I had no idea if I was being told the truth or if someone else was covering their ass. Everyone was playing pin the tail on the donkey. I was the new donkey.

Then there were the high-frequency radios and the non-directional beacon that was out there. Some idiot added those to my inventory without paperwork. According to the Army, they were not available to any of our units.

The final nail in my coffin came when the Colonel called me in and reminded me that we were due for an IG inspection next month, maybe later, but soon. IG is short for Inspector General. Now I was like a cat in a sandbox trying to cover up everyone else's shit... and my own.

Finally, in desperation, I reached out for help. Probably the dumbest thing I could have done. But I was desperate at this point and couldn't see any other way. I needed expert help or advice. Dumb or not, I didn't care. I called Regimental Headquarters in Nha Trang and got in touch with a Chief Warrant Officer W-4. That was the highest rank available as a Warrant Officer at that time.

Warrant officers were just what they were called. They were enlisted men whose expertise warranted officer status, but not an officer in the traditional sense. A W-4 could walk on water. They usually sat at the Commander's table in the mess hall. In the States, they had their own parking spot. They were a big deal. Being a W-4 was a huge deal.

After explaining my situation, he told me to stop what I was doing and not touch anything else. "Leave everything as you have it right now. I'll be down tomorrow to look at everything myself, and I'll let you know what can be done."

This is where it gets surreal. At the beginning of this book, I told you I would tell the truth, the whole truth, and nothing but the truth. So I'm telling you again. Trust me, this is too weird not to be true. I swear.

He arrived around 9 or 10am the following day and opened by asking me for the property books. He spent a couple hours going through them and then asked me for the "Grand Tour." We walked and talked until late that afternoon. Finally, late in the evening, he called me into my office, which he had commandeered, and asked me to sit down.

"Is that mortar in the arms room on the books anywhere?" I told him that it wasn't, I hadn't found any record of it. I explained that it was still there because I didn't know how to safely dispose of it. That's when he began to hatch his new plan.

I could feel myself being sucked into another shit storm, maybe bigger than the one I was already in. But what choice did I have? I listened to his proposal.

"Do you think you could arrange a direct hit between those two filing cabinets during your next alert?"

It took me a few seconds, but I was beginning to see where he was headed. "Sure," I said.

"No one gets hurt, understand?"

"Yes, Sir," I said. He wasn't a "sir," but I called him sir anyway.

"No one gets hurt, no fires, no other damage, if possible."

"Yes, sir."

"Call me when that happens, and I'll come back down. Maybe a week from now? Just make sure it hits right here between these two filing cabinets." And he pointed at the space between them and looked at me to be sure I was listening. "You need to hurry. That's important. Understand?" and he stood up and walked out.

We hadn't had an alert in weeks. The last attack on our base had been when that "sniper" shot two holes into the Red Cross trailer. We would have to create our own attack, and I needed someone who knew more about that rocket than I did. I decided to get my supply sergeant involved. I was running out of time. I needed his help. But first, I needed to find out if I could trust him.

After thinking it over, I decided I had no choice except to trust him. He seems like a decent guy. He and I were becoming friends, as much as enlisted men and officers could be friends.

That evening, my sergeant and I started setting up our plan. Once we were both in agreement and the plan was made, my sergeant assured me that he knew what he was doing. Finally, he told me that he thought I should leave. "Go to your quarters and wait," were his last words to me. My last words were, "No one gets hurt, right?" "Right, sir. Go."

That evening I lay in bed trying to sleep but couldn't. I was too afraid that something would go wrong... that someone would be hurt... or that my sergeant would blow up half the compound. But he didn't.

My sergeant, bless his heart, put a hand grenade between the two filing cabinets and set it to go off when he pulled a piece of twine he had attached to the pin. He waited until no one was in sight, yanked the pin out, and stepped back around the corner.

It ripped both filing cabinets almost in half. It started a small fire that quickly died out. Still, it left enough embers to maintain that the embers belonged to the property books and all the other documents in the files.

Sweet success! We could finally call our CWO in Nha Trang and let him know we were ready.

He arrived the next day and made a visual inspection. He looked at me and asked where I hid the real property books. I'm not sure how he knew I kept them, but I told him, and he asked me to bring them to him and then leave him to his work. "Lock the door on your way out."

Chief was there for two full days working by himself in my office. He left to eat, relieve himself, and sleep, but other than that, he sat in my chair and worked. He mainly worked with my sergeant. He knew now that the Sergeant had been the one who pulled the pin on that grenade, so he trusted him.

He would call him in, ask for something he needed, lock the door, and go back to work. "Bring me a list of all your weapons and who they are assigned to." This went on for two days.

Finally, when he finished, he called my sergeant and me into my office. He spent the next two hours showing us how to properly post entries into a property book. When that was finished, his final words were for me not to acquire any more unauthorized equipment while I was in Vietnam. Then he handed me a "honey-do" list and said, "Have this done in the next two weeks." He wasn't asking. "All of it, understand?" Then he said the obvious, "There is no reason that you two should suffer for what the Colonel should have taken care of long before it got out of control. There is no reason for either of you to lose rank, or worse, because of poor leadership." Finally, someone said the unsayable.

No one ever questioned what had happened during those two weeks. That bothered me more than if the Colonel had called me and grilled me again for three hours. Something always goes wrong with a plan to deceive. It's just a matter of how big they were. If the screw-ups were too small to be noticed, that would be one thing. If they were too big to ignore, that was another, but something always goes wrong when you're in a sandbox covering up shit.

The next day, I got an invitation to play in the poker game. That was a good sign. Only the Colonels inner circle got to play in that game. The first thing I thought of when I sat down was, "Where's the duck?"

There is always a duck that gets invited to a poker game. I looked around and saw two possibilities, but I wasn't sure. Finally, after playing for ten minutes, I knew who the ducks were; in this game, it wasn't me. Maybe three of the six players at the table were poker players, and the rest were ducks. I was finally accepted as one of the good guys. Life was good again. I don't know how the Colonel knew, but he had to guess something was going on when that Chief Warrant Officer sat in my office for two days. Maybe that's all he wanted to know. He probably assumed I had found a way to keep us out of trouble. Somehow, he was starting to put two and two together, and it wasn't adding up to three anymore. That's all he wanted to know.

Chapter 26: The Inspector General

A month had passed since the explosion, and still, there was no sign of the dreaded IG team. The longer, the better, I kept telling my sergeant. Then, one day, bright and early, there they were. Coming out of the Colonel's office and walking straight toward me was my CWO4. He was going to be my IG inspector. Each member of his team peeled off and went to their respective areas, one by one. Even Capt. Pilgrim was greeted by one of them. I noticed a little bead of sweat running down Pilgram's cheek when he shook hands with his inspector.

To make a long story short, I received several dings. I expected that. Everyone does. I'd been through too many inspections before this one. I expected to get some criticisms. I knew that there was no such thing as perfect in the Army, certainly not from me. The Chief wrote down my shortcomings and talked with me about each one. He wasn't pleased with what we had done "remodeling" the arms room. He wanted the rifle racks bolted to the floor. It was chained. This went on for three hours, and then he thanked me and walked back to the Colonel's office. He was soon joined by the rest of his team. It was over. I hadn't been arrested on the spot. Now, I had to wait, along with all the others, for our scores. It would take days before I finally got my score for supply.

We were all called into the Colonel's office when the dreaded day finally arrived. He was going to bar-bque each of us in public. He would do it one at a time for everyone to see. Capt. Pilgrim was there, and all the Colonel's staff were there. One by one, the Colonel reviewed the results of each department. The first thing I noticed was that nothing was said to Signal about the high-frequency radios.

He covered each department one by one, and finally, it was my turn. "Last but not least, our Battalion Supply Officer scored the highest score ever given to a field unit in Vietnam. Congratulations, Lt. Speed."

Here's what felt the weirdest of all, it actually looked like he meant it. He was as surprised as I was... no, not surprised, shocked as I was. I don't think he knew what we had done, the Chief and me. He was expecting one of us, himself, Pilgrim, or me, to end up in jail or something worse. At the very least, one of us would get a reprimand.

The son of a bitch didn't know how I pulled it off. It had been days since the inspection, and I could still see the relief on his face. He didn't know.

A month later, I was promoted to Captain... two weeks before I was eligible. There had been those who said that my career was over. They were wrong. My career wouldn't be over until I said it was over.

Chapter 27: Going Home with a

Passenger

I was going to make a new friend. The headmistress of the Red Cross ladies came to me one afternoon and asked if I would escort one of her girls to the Officer's Mess for dinner one evening. She explained, "She goes to work every day, and when she gets off, she comes straight back to our trailer. She's been here for two months and is still too shy to do her job as well as she could if she got more involved. She comes from a prominent family. She attended the best schools. She volunteered for duty in Vietnam, but she hasn't been able to make new friends here. I think she is frightened to death to be here." She looked at me and frowned, "I trust you will honor your position as an officer and a gentleman and not take advantage of her situation." I nodded in agreement, and I meant it. Based on what she told me, I felt sorry for the young lady.

This was the beginning of a special relationship. One like I've never experienced before or after. I had a completely platonic relationship with this lady. Seeing her as anything other than my best friend never dawned on me. We spent hours together each week. I escorted her to the beach in Cam Ranh. We even sat in my quarters one night and drank wine. She was a lady, and I treated her as such.

She was my best friend and nothing more. It never occurred to me to want more than that from her. After all, she was a lady, and I was a gentleman. Mine might have taken an act of Congress to achieve. But I did have a document stating that I was an officer and a gentleman. And it was signed by the President of the United States. Crazy helicopter pilot or not. I had proof.

I played poker two or three times a week. When I was not in a poker game or at work, I was with Jodie. Finally, my life was making sense again. I was happy. It was time to ask the Army to let me go home.

I learned how I made Captain two weeks earlier than I was eligible. I scored the highest score in a field supply unit IG inspection. It wasn't because I was better than everyone else. It was because I was resourceful, plus I was lucky. All these months in Vietnam, someone had been watching over me. Protecting me from myself. I had been an instrument of death for dozens of people on my aircraft without ever getting a scratch myself. Not one. Good fortune was wearing me like it owned me, and I didn't like it. I couldn't put my finger on it, but I was different. Later, when I talked about that feeling, my friend told me that war did that to people. That I couldn't go into my war and come out the same person I was before. He was right, but it was more than that. I couldn't figure it out. There was something else going on.

Once again, I did what I shouldn't have. I sat down and wrote a letter to my Congressman. Since I could no longer fly, I wanted to be released from my flight school obligation. I had served my six-year obligation. I wanted to go home. Not the kind of wanting to go home that the teenagers just arriving wanted. I had done my part. I had faced more than the enemy. I had faced my own weaknesses and continued to fight. Now, I was growing tired of war. My tour in Vietnam would be over soon, and I wanted to stop being a soldier. I spelled it all out in that letter to the same Congressman that my father said had been ready to sponsor me for consideration for the Naval Academy. I laid my soul out for everyone to see, ending with my stupid attempt at suicide.

It would take months for my request to reach someone who would or could act on it. My tour in Vietnam was almost over, and I already had my new orders to Fort Carson, Colorado. These are probably the best orders I could have asked for. But I wanted out. Not because I no longer saw myself as a patriot but because I did. I had done everything the Army had asked me to do and more. I'm not sure I can explain it. It was different now. I was different now. I no longer believed in what we were doing in Vietnam. I would continue to follow my orders and obey my superiors, but not like before. Something was broken inside, and I didn't know how to fix it.

Then, days before I was due to rotate, the officer in charge of personnel asked me to come to his office. My orders had been changed. I was going to leave in two days for out-processing in Oakland, California. From there, I would be flown back to Pensacola, Florida. "Opieville was a mere 5 miles from Pensacola. I could walk from the airport to my parent's house if I needed to. My wife would be there with Michael and Ivy, my two children. I could hold them and kiss them any time I wanted. It would finally be over, or so I thought.

Little did I know it was just beginning. I was going home with an uninvited guest tagging along. I had a passenger sitting next to me; he would be there for the rest of my life. I had PTSD. I didn't know that then. It would take years for me to realize what was wrong. It took years to figure out why I no longer trusted the people in positions of authority. But it was more than that. I didn't trust anyone. **I thought that I could walk on water, and all that time, I was drowning.**

Chapter 28: The Most Difficult Chapter to Talk About

Unless you have Combat-related PTSD, you probably will not understand my hesitancy to talk about it. It's like any other mental disorder. People look at "crazy people" and judge them. You've done it all your life. I think that it is a normal reaction. We're trained from birth to avoid people who are different than us. Our mothers called them strangers.

"Don't talk to strangers." "Don't get in a car with a stranger." It's a healthy, learned response from our childhood. It's part of our fight-or-flight response system. You don't run from something until you have a concern about it. So, please understand I am not being critical of you for judging or being concerned about people with PTSD. It's normal.

Every time we meet someone, we make a snap judgment about them. It happens whether you think about it or not. It's how our brains work. Why am I spending so much time on this? I want you to understand that it happens to everyone and that it is okay. Go ahead and judge people like me, but do it with a degree of understanding.

PTSD, Post Traumatic Stress Disorder, has many causes. I'm here to talk about the one I know intimately: combat-related PTSD. There are as many types of PTSD as there are people that have it. Everyone is different. But there are some common symptoms.

Substance abuse, anxiety or mood disorders, increased sensitivity of the fight or flight responses, increased sensitivity to other traumatic events, hypervigilance, and avoiding other stressful activities such as large groups of people. Avoiding trigger activities, any activity that reminds us of what caused our disorder. Flashbacks and nightmares. These are all biggies.

If the Veterans Administration has rated you 100% disabled with PTSD, you have entered new territory. I've never seen it, but I'm told that the VA has a two-inch thick manual that describes the symptoms needed for a rating of less than 100%. There are only two pages that give the criterion for 100%. Remember all those suicides that I wrote about? That's part of it.

I will wrap this chapter up with some advice for my fellow PTSD sufferers. Then, I will get on with my story. The best treatment for PTSD is admitting that you have it and accepting it. Learn to live with it. Stop trying to hide it or from it.

Be like the one-legged ass-kicker and realize that you are never going to win that ass-kicking contest that everyone keeps talking about. So move on with your life. Live life as best you can and enjoy as much of it as possible.

This chapter could go on for hours, but I can't hold your attention that long. So, I'm going to stop here and say that PTSD is disabling and currently impossible to cure. It can be treated, but here again, everyone is different. Treatment usually requires years of mental therapy combined with drug therapy before it is effective enough to allow your PTSD to go unnoticed.

I am not a physician, but I am writing from personal experience. Part of this is me repeating things I have been told by so-called experts. Part of it is from what I have learned from personal experience.

When you judge what I write from here on, remember this. You can't understand what living with PTSD is like until you have lived it. I live it every day.

I'm just trying to give you a peek. More would be wasted because you would lack that personal knowledge I spoke of.

Chapter 29: Coming Home

I arrived in Oakland and was processed out. To her credit, my wife was there. So, I had high hopes that we would be able to work things out.

Many of my friends talk about what they went through coming home through Oakland. But, unlike what they experienced, no one spat on me. There weren't any protesters there that day to boo me. None of that happened to me. But it was strange, nevertheless. I was in uniform, and people looked at me differently than when I boarded my flight out of Pensacola a year before.

There weren't any crowds there welcoming me home, either. That was a little disappointing. But, somewhere in the back of my mind, I remembered those newsreels when my dad's generation came home. That would have helped me readjust to the "real world" I had heard so much about. I don't think I expected it, but in retrospect, it was odd.

My wife flew to Oakland and welcomed me home. My parents and my children were there when I arrived in

Pensacola. Of course, I was happy to be back. But in the back of my mind, I kept remembering those newsreels.

Even when I returned to Pensacola, the welcoming committees weren't there. Pensacola was a military town, and no one came up to me and thanked me for my service or said welcome home. I couldn't help but notice that my war differed from my dad's. I had to wonder, was the time he gave in service to his country better than mine? Were his sacrifices bigger than mine? It just seemed odd to me. But I let it go. I was home. I think that later, I would realize that when I let it go, "it" didn't let go of me.

When I took off my uniform, I stopped talking about Vietnam. That part of my life was over, and I was ready to move on. It was time to stop thinking about my war and comparing it to my expectations. Or comparing it to my dad's war.

Except once, when during a job interview, I noticed that the guy I was talking to was once a pilot in the military. I told him that I flew helicopters in the Army. I think that swayed him. He hired me. He was a pilot during World War II. I sucked at the job he hired me for, and we parted later, but I'm getting ahead of myself here.

Back home in Pensacola, I felt out of place. I didn't have anything in common with my friends at church. Most of them were either married or had moved away. My friends during high school and I had nothing in common... nothing at all. I remember talking to one of them and thinking he was different than when we had known each other six years earlier.

That's the irony of it all. I thought they were different, not me. It took years for me to figure that one out.

I went to church a few times. That was part of the agreement I made with Brenda, my wife. She wanted me to start going to church again. She wanted me to set a good example for my two children. I knew she was right, but in my heart, I felt out of place at church.

I was having a crisis of faith. How do you explain something like that to a fellow Mormon? For them, faith was everything. Bearing one's testimony was an act of faith that we each did once a month. It had been years since I bore my testimony. It was starting to show.

I went in one Sunday and asked to speak to the Branch President at church. I needed to talk to someone about how I was feeling. I didn't understand what was happening to me, but looking back, I probably had a panic attack. He was busy and sat down with me and explained that he couldn't talk with me then, but he took the time to tell me that I shouldn't worry about it. Instead, I should pray about it. Then he talked about what a good leader I had been before and how he expected great things from me in the future. He left minutes after he sat down. That was the last time I went to church, that I remember. Maybe once or twice later, when I visited my mother and dad in Seminary, Mississippi.

Even there, I felt out of place. I was there because I didn't want to embarrass my family. I smelled like smoke. I was smoking back then. I always smoked when I was under pressure. Going home to see Mom and Dad caused more anxiety than anything I did. I didn't want to disappoint them, but there I was.

After returning to Pensacola, I decided to move to Jacksonville, Florida. The funny thing about that move is that I don't remember talking to Brenda about it. It was closer to her parents. I guess I just assumed she wouldn't mind. It was just one of the times that I realized that was different now. It was happening more now than before. I'm not saying that it was a bad thing. People change. They grow. I just didn't feel any bigger or better. If I was growing... how was I changing and why?

That's when I took the job in Jacksonville with the Navy pilot I mentioned earlier. He was one of the owners of E.H. Thompson Hotel and Restaurant Supply Company. The guy genuinely liked me. He gave me the job the day we met.

My job was to drive around to all the restaurants and bars between Ocala and Jacksonville and sell bar and restaurant supplies. Anything from complete kitchens to a few spoons and knives. We had a design center to handle the large accounts. In those cases, my job was to report back and let them send their designer in.

I will not be able to explain how I screwed up that job. I'm not sure I know what was in my head then. I couldn't concentrate on doing it. I spent more time looking for old cars than I did selling restaurant supplies. That probably was from my days flying around the Brazos with Mr. Toth and looking in those old barns and sheds.

When I left Jacksonville, I left a 1933 four-door LaSalle Sedan and a '35 Auburn model 635 four-door convertible sitting in the driveway. They were cars that needed to be restored. When I bought them, I thought I could sell them and make a few hundred on each of them. I never got around to doing that.

I think that the only thing of value that I found was a baby raccoon in Fernandina Beach Park. It was maybe a few days old when I saw it lying on the yellow stripe in the middle of an asphalt road. I could close my hand and hide it completely, tail and all. She was a she, didn't open her eyes for a week or so. The kids loved her. I could write a chapter on her alone, but I won't. We named her Bandit because of her mask.

I'm avoiding writing what I need to say here. Instead, I need to fast forward a few months.

While I worked at E.H. Thompson Hotel and Restaurant Supply, one of the bars I called on hired me to work weekends as a bouncer and bartender. They needed someone to help keep everyone civil and work the service bar. My job was to help keep the waitresses supplied and caught up. It was a busy place. Every county above that one was a dry county. It was the closest bar for about half of the lower part of Georgia. The Playbill catered to the Redneck crowds. I didn't need to know how to mix drinks. It was strictly a shot and beer kind of joint.

My job was to take care of the waitresses, but I had four stools that customers could sit on when the place was packed. No space was wasted. It was always packed at the Playbill Bar and Lounge. The owner offered me more to work two nights a week than I was making working all week at E.H. Thompson. It was a no-brainer. I needed the money.

One night, we were so busy that we didn't get cleaned up until an hour after we closed. Everyone decided we should go to Callahan, Florida, and have breakfast at the all-night diner. I had a couple of drinks with the others after we closed. I wasn't drunk by any means, but I did have a few drinks. I was the last one to arrive at the diner.

In those days, I had a bad habit of leaving my keys under my seat and not locking my car. I don't remember why I did it. I just did.

The local sheriff stopped me just as I opened the front door at the diner. He asked me if I had been drinking? I didn't lie. I said yes. I wasn't anywhere near drunk, so I thought nothing of it. He grabbed me and cuffed me. Then, he told me that I was under arrest for drunk driving.

I thought that he was being funny, and I laughed. That pissed him off, I guess. Next, he asked me where I parked my car? I refused to tell him. Then, he asked me what kind of car I was driving? What year was it? What color was it? Each time I refused to answer him, he got a little more upset. He was an ass. If anyone ever needed a replacement for Boss Hogg, he was their man.

The town there was well known for arresting people after they left the Playbill. That was the name of the bar where I worked. In fact, a few years later, the State of Florida took its city charter, and the sheriff went to prison. My boss at the Playbill had warned me that the sheriff was known for arresting people and impounding their vehicles. He told me to be careful when I was in Callahan. Being careful didn't help. He didn't know what kind of car I was driving, and he still arrested me for driving while intoxicated. Ironic.

The Sheriff had a scam where he arrested people and forced them to pay a cash fine to get out of jail. When he turned them loose, their car would be at the impound lot, and they were charged towing and lot fees. It would cost you two hundred dollars to get out of Callahan, and they didn't take checks. Cash only. That's what they got the Sheriff on. Tax evasion.

He decided to let me spend the night or stay until I told him what car I was driving. The diner was always packed on the weekends, and their parking lot was full of cars. The sheriff couldn't figure out which car was mine, and I didn't have the keys to give it away. I ended up spending the night in jail.

Sunday morning, he let me call my wife and ask her to bring two hundred dollars to bail me out. She didn't have two hundred in cash. (My rent on a lovely three-bedroom cinder-block home in a nice subdivision back then was $125) Two hundred dollars was a lot of money. We could eat well on two hundred dollars for two months... All four of us.

As I said, Brenda didn't have two hundred dollars in cash, so she went to my boss, who gave her the money. But he told her to tell me not to come back in. I could keep the $200. He fired me.

Brenda left me and went to live with her mother in Valdosta. I waited for three days and went after her. I must admit. She gave me a fair warning.

I was making as much money working at the Playbill as I was at E.H. Thompson, so I stayed there while I looked for a new job.

One night at work, this guy was getting rowdy, and one of the waitresses sat him at my bar to cool off. Of course, everyone knew that I was the bouncer, and he took offense. He was acting like an ass. He pounded on the bar and demanded service even though he could plainly see a dozen people in front of him.

After sitting there for a few minutes and drinking a few beers, he decided he'd had enough. He yelled at me and threatened me. I probably handled it wrong. I ignored him. I was too busy to stop. He jumped over the bar and tried to grab me. He took a swing at me, and I hit him once. It was a good one. I clocked the bastard.

After he had been out for a half-hour, the owner called an ambulance. Someone else called the sheriff. My boss said that it wasn't him. The sheriff didn't have a problem with what I did. Everyone told him that I had only hit the guy once and that he had started it. I heard one lady say something that didn't bother the sheriff, but it did bother me. She said, "He didn't look mad or upset. He was just defending himself." The "he" she was talking about was me.

She was right. I wasn't upset. I realized that I wasn't upset by what I did. I didn't care. I was smart enough to know that wasn't right. I wasn't smart enough to care. Or I couldn't. I don't know which. As we said in Vietnam, it was what it was.

Later, the sheriff told me that the guy was still out and that I should leave before he had to take me in and make a statement. I told the sheriff that the guy was drunk out of his skull and probably needed to sleep it off.

My boss at the Playbill fired me. He gave me a couple hundred dollars as a parting gift and thanked me for my help. Once again, I went home without a job.

I never heard what happened to the guy.

Brenda wasn't happy. This time, she didn't go home to her mother. She asked me to leave. But she said something that I took offense to. She said that she didn't want me around the kids. She said that I was a bad influence on them. She wanted me to leave and not come back.

That day, I bought a one-year-old used Honda 350cc Scrambler from the Honda motorcycle dealer. They told me that the previous owner added a larger rear sprocket and that it would climb straight up. Other than that, it was like new. I liked it. I signed the papers and drove it home. I packed what I needed to survive and left that afternoon.

Chapter 30: Road Trip

It was mid-September and still hot weather in Florida. It was cool in the evenings but still hot in the afternoon. I made it as far as Tallahassee before I blew out my rear tire. It was late afternoon and too late to look for a tire shop on foot. In those days, everything closed at dark... and on Sundays. I don't remember what day it was. I mentioned Sundays because that was back when everyone closed at six, just as everyone who had a job got off work. I always felt that businesses were catering to the unemployed back then. Anyone who had a job had to be at work. Back then, the old Blue laws determined who could be open on Sundays.

I was going about 65 miles per hour when my rear tire blew out. The tire folded first to one side, and the bike's rear started tracking in that direction. Then it worked its way to the other side, and the rear was tracking in the opposite direction.

The rear end of the bike was trying to outrun the front end. It was hairy until I got the Honda down to twenty mph or something close and stopped. It blew a hole in the innertube that could never be patched and shredded the tire. It was almost dark, so the only thing that I could do was look for a place to camp out for the night.

The following day, I woke up looking at the business end of a shotgun. Three black men were standing there. One was holding a sawed-off shotgun, and one was holding my duffle bag. Then I saw my attaché case in the third guy's hand. Every legal document I owned was in the attaché case. I had planned to drop those off in Pensacola with my folks. Instead, these guys took my DD214, clothes, artic flight jacket, and money. The guy with the shotgun asked for my wallet. I gave it to him. Why not. They had everything else.

I did talk him into leaving the wallet. I asked him to take the money and leave me the credit card and driver's license. He obliged. Now, I had a Phillips 66 credit card with a $200 limit, my driver's license, and the clothes I had on. So far, I had almost been killed when my bike blew out the rear tire. I'd been robbed of everything of value that I owned. This was turning into the trip from hell, and I'd only gone 150 miles.

The next day, I found a tire store, and they sold me a new tire and innertube and accepted my Phillips 66 credit card. It was the first time that I used it. I wasn't sure they would take it. Thank goodness I had my driver's license to prove who I was. That's the only thing they asked me for when they took my card to pay for the tire.

I made it to Pensacola around three that afternoon. I spent most of the day explaining to my mother why I was leaving Brenda and my children. I don't think that my mom could wrap her head around the fact that Brenda asked me to leave. Dad surprised me. He didn't ask me what was going on. When I think back, I think he knew.

Mother tried to talk me into staying with them, but she relented when I explained that I wanted to take some time off and thought this would be good for me. Again, Dad surprised me. He took me out and bought me a change of clothes, 2 three packs of underwear and a jacket. He handed me 2 one-hundred-dollar bills, neatly folded, and said, "Be careful, Hoss."

Oh, I forgot. The three black pulp-wood cutters that robbed me left me my flight helmet and the sleeping bag that I was lying in when they robbed me. Plus, I had an Army blanket in the sleeping bag. I still had those, plus that night, I went to bed fully dressed, boots and all. That's just about everything that I had left. I would be traveling light from here on.

The bike I was riding had a few shortcomings. One was the 150-mile limit because of the size of the fuel tank. I mentioned the other big problem before. The larger sprocket meant that at full throttle, wide open, I was going about 65 mph. I wasn't sure because my speedometer wasn't working right. The speed limit in those days was 70 in most places and 75 in others. Full throttle meant I was working the hell out of the engine and putting a lot of pressure on my tailpipes.

I made it to Vicksburg that night and spent my third night there.

I found one more factor in how far I could travel each day. Scrambler was just another word for a dirt bike back then. Scramblers weren't made for the highway or long trips. They rattled your brains. After three hours, I'd have to stop and get the blood circulating in my arms and hands again. I'd walk around, trying to get my butt cheeks to un-cramp. Then, I was back on my bike, looking for another service station that would accept my Phillips 66 card. I got lucky. I don't remember its name, but the big motel that sits almost under the Mississippi River bridge as you leave

Vicksburg accepted Phillips 66 credit cards. I had shrimp for supper that night and rented a room.

Going across Louisiana, the weather started cooling. My jacket was more of a windbreaker than a jacket. It was a Florida-weight jacket. I improvised, cut a hole in the middle of my wool Army blanket, and wore it like a poncho. It worked great. It blocked the wind, and it kept me warm. It also caught fire crossing Texas when the baffles blew out of my tailpipes and turned them into trumpets. They glowed red hot from then on.

When the baffles blew, it sounded like someone pulled the trigger on a double-barreled shotgun. The first one blew, then the other one blew moments later. They were flame red, and they were sailing into traffic behind me. Cars were swerving, trying not to get hit. I almost laughed, but some of those cars were catching up to me, and one was wagging a finger at me.

He was trying to tell me that my poncho was on fire.

Somewhere between Tyler, Texas, and Dallas, I ran out of luck and gas at the same time. This was back in 1969. The Interstate was still considered new. There wasn't much of anything between Tyler and Dallas. So far as I could tell, there weren't any Phillips 66 truck stops.

I-10 was so new then that parts of downtown Dallas were still unfinished. While pushing that dirt bike, I took off my poncho and jacket. I remember wishing it was as cool while pushing that damned thing as it had been riding it. One long hill after another was all I could see in my future.

Once again, my luck changed. A pickup truck with a topper pulled off the road in front of me. Two young boys started running back and helped me push my Honda to their truck. I saw two stripped-down dirt bikes when they opened the bed cover and tailgate. I recognized them as bikes set up for indoor dirt tracks. Trust me. You will know an indoor dirt bike when you see it.

The boys moved their bikes around and made room for one more. Then helped me lift my bike into the bed. One stayed in the back, and the other told me to join him and his dad inside. They were on their way to a dirt bike indoor stadium. The dad rode the 500cc, and one of his boys rode the smaller bike. I don't remember what size the kid's bike was.

After talking for a while, the guy asked me about my flight helmet. When I told him I was a helicopter pilot in Vietnam, I had my homecoming. First, they took me with them to race their bikes. Then, he bought me some hotdogs and drinks. After the races, they invited me to go home with them and spend the night. I thought that this guy was the nicest guy I had ever met.

The following day, they let me sleep in. I got up around eight or nine in the morning. We hadn't gone to bed until one or two that morning. Breakfast was waiting, plus he had made two sandwiches for me to take with me. He had a soda and the two sandwiches in a paper bag tied to the suitcase Dad and Mom gave me in Pensacola. Then he told me everything he did to my bike while I slept in. He had changed the oil, tuned it up, fixed several small things, and put baffles back in the mufflers. When I asked how much I owed him. He shook my hand and said that it was his gift to me. Then he said it all. "I'm happy to help a fellow veteran. I wish I could go with you."

It's been over fifty years since that happened. I remember it like it was yesterday. That's good for me. I'm surprised when I can remember the code on my debit card.

Gas was cheap back then. I stopped often and filled up. Most of it was around 25 cents a gallon. The lowest I paid was 19.9 cents a gallon in one of the suburbs of Ft. Worth. Going across Texas was a challenge. I slept on a roadside park bench one night. It was a covered area. That was good. It rained that night.

This one will be hard to believe, but as before, I swear it's true. One night, I drove too long. I was trying to get a little farther down the road. I remember seeing a sign saying this town was 12 miles ahead of me. I had enough gas to go that far, but I would cut it short for anything after that.

By the way, I forgot to mention that my scrambler didn't have a gas gauge, and the speedometer stopped working right after I left Fort Worth. The speedo wasn't any great loss. With the larger sprocket, it was way off anyway. I was sure I was okay and could get gas in that town. There was a big truck stop there.

I watched for it, but the town never showed up. I had been down this highway several times and remembered the truck stop. Then I saw road signs on the other side of the highway, and for some reason, I decided to see how far back the last town was. The sign said that it was 10 miles to Alvord. That was the name of the town I was going to stop in. I had driven through the town and not known it. I tried to remember where I had been. The best I can tell, I was either asleep or mesmerized. Or something. I turned around and went back. The town was lit up like a Christmas tree. Especially the truck stop. Somehow, I'd missed it.

I slept under a bridge that night. That wasn't a choice. It was all that was available without turning around and going back to the last town.

Going across Texas, I pulled off the road and played in the sand with my dirt bike several times. It was a great country for off-roading. Rolling hills and washes everywhere. It would surprise you to know everything I saw riding off-road in Texas. I saw a shitload of snakes and more old trucks than I could count. Most of the trucks were in washes.

I used some of my medic training up around Bowie, Texas. This husband and wife team was driving an almost new Thunderbird. It was one of the big, heavy ones. I think he fell asleep at the wheel and ran off the road. When he tried to jerk it back on, he flipped it right down the middle of the highway. I was the second person on the scene.

The first car that stopped was a lady in her forties. (I'm guessing) She was trying to help the old lady. The T-bird was upside down, and the driver was sitting on what was once the roof but was now the floor. He was obviously in shock and looked banged up. But what bothered me most was that he had a v-shaped cut on his forehead, and it was hanging away from his skull. It wasn't bleeding as much as I thought it should, but I asked him to hold his hand over it and hold it in place.

Other than trying to keep him awake and have him hold his handkerchief over that flap, there wasn't much more that I could do. I tried to keep the guy talking. I was worried that he might pass out and hurt himself falling. It looked like he could have a few broken bones, but I was most worried that he might have had a concussion. If he didn't, it would be a miracle. He didn't look much better than his car, and it bent to hell to and back.

This was pre-cellphones. We flagged down a car going back toward the last town and asked them to stop and tell the police to send an ambulance. I waited until I heard sirens coming. Now, there were several cars there, and people were trying to help. When I heard the sirens, I returned to my bike and left.

What is the point of this story? If you ever find yourself in that kind of trouble, pray that a veteran with PTSD stops. I knew what to do and what not to do. But my way of helping that day was staying calm and keeping my head on straight. It's difficult to convince an injured person that they will be okay if you're scaring them. Some of the people who stopped were doing just that. They were shouting and running around like a bunch of weirdos. I was in the zone. For me, everything was happening in slow motion, and I stayed clear-headed. I think I made a difference that day. It felt good to be in control of my emotions again. Even if it was just for those few minutes.

I spent a couple more days getting to Colorado. The closer to Colorado I got, the colder the weather got. Finally, maybe fifty miles before Kit Carson, it started snowing. I checked... it was still September. I don't think I have ever been that cold in my life. Plus, riding a motorcycle on ice and snow ain't no party.

By the time I pulled into Kit Carson, Colorado, the roads had at least ten inches of snow on them, and ice was starting to form under the snow. The sand trucks and snowplows were still in the C-dot garages. No one had expected this one. No one could remember the last blizzard this early in September. Sure, a little snow in the high country, but not a blizzard in the flat lands? I made it to the only service station open anywhere. The little motel across the street from the service station was packed.

The service station owner wanted to go home. I was standing in front of his Franklin wood-burning stove, trying to thaw out. After an hour or so, a truck stopped to buy gas. The station owner ran out and asked him if he would give me a ride into Denver. The driver was a medic, or nurse, at Fitzsimmons Army Hospital. He was driving a nearly new El Camino, and he said yes.

If you think riding a motorcycle in the snow is dangerous, try doing it in an El Camino. Rear-wheel drive and no weight in the back on the drive wheels. We were slipping and sliding all over the highway. But we made it to Aurora. A trip that would typically take two hours took six hours. He let me out at the Riviera Motel. He helped me get my bike out without scratching up his bed any more than I already had. I thanked him, and he left.

31: Getting It Together

Let me count the ways that I loved the Riviera Motel. First and foremost, they took Phillips 66 credit cards. Second and almost as important, they had a nice bar and it was a hang-out for student nurses from Fitzsimmons VA Hospital. But the biggest reason was when they discovered my Phillips 66 card was used up a few days later, and I still owed money. They didn't call the police. They did cut it in half before they handed it back to me. The blizzard was over, but the streets were still impassable. They told me to drive carefully. There was still icy slush on the highways. I think they had grown fond of me. In those few days, I decided that I liked Denver and decided to stay... At least for a while.

I remembered that Jodie Rouse was from Denver. So I decided to call her and say hello. She was in California. She was working in a VA burn center and lived there. I called the Red Cross and asked if I could have her address. I didn't know it then, but they called her parents and alerted them that an ex-Army soldier was looking for their daughter. It took her dad and a private detective three months to find me. When he did, I was invited to his home for supper. After supper, we drank Wild Turkey and looked at photographs Jodie sent home, showing her and me together. Jodie's dad was a blast. I don't think her mother was all that impressed with our behavior. When Mr. Rouse called Jodie, and he and I talked to her, I don't think she was impressed either. It was not my finest hour. That was the last time that I talked to Miss Rouse.

An odd thing happens when you drive into Denver Proper at night. Highway 287 comes out of Ft. Worth and runs north to Limon, Colorado. I don't know if it still does. Still, at one time, it turned into the main drag, Colfax Avenue. Colfax ran through Aurora,

Denver, and Lakewood and on into the mountains. So if you do like I did and come into Aurora at night, you never realize that you're not driving north.

Somewhere around Limon, Colfax zigs, then zags and turns West. I might have been asleep when the El Camino left Limon.

As an old pilot, I could always tell you which way north was. I spent 30-plus years in Denver looking for the mountains to figure out where I was. West was North in my internal compass. I never got over that.

Worse yet, there was a huge arch that said welcome to Aurora. There are no signs saying that you just left Aurora and entered Denver. No signs saying that you've left Denver and are in Lakewood. For all I knew, Aurora ran from Fitzsimmons to Golden and the foothills. It happened to me, and I've heard others say the same thing. For the longest time I thought Aurora was the biggest city in the world.

Aurora was the largest city in Colorado at that time. Denver was second, and Lakewood was third. That was then. Now Denver is first, Colorado Springs is second, and Aurora is third. Things change, and cities grow. By the time you read this it might change again.

I arrived in Denver without a dime to my name. I was homeless and broke. After my Phillips 66 card died, I went days without eating. Eventually, I sold my Honda and answered an ad in the newspaper about a place to live. A guy named Bob Ward wanted a roommate to help him with his rent. He lived in a townhouse on Green Mountain. I could sit and look out our window and see all of Denver below. On a clear night, there is no more beautiful city than Denver at night. It never grew old.

One day, Robert and his girlfriend came into my room and talked with me. His girlfriend at the time was a nurse. I didn't know it then, but Bob brought her home that night to check on me. Bob said I hadn't been out of my room in a month. I asked him how I ate. He said that he brought sandwiches every time I asked for one. Bob said that after a while, he got worried and asked his girlfriend to come and talk with me. When I looked confused, Bob's girlfriend asked me to look at myself in the mirror. I didn't recognize myself. I was skin and bones skinny.

Bob's nurse asked me if I was hungry. I couldn't remember my last meal, but I wasn't hungry. She wanted me to come downstairs and eat. Before I could agree, she told me that I had to bathe before she would feed me. I was a little crusty. I looked in the mirror and could see why she was concerned. I hadn't shaved in months, and my beard hadn't ever been shaped. I looked like the wild man from Borneo. I smelled the same way.

Later that day, Bob's nurse gave me a haircut and trimmed my beard. Someone washed my clothes. It was probably her. With food in my stomach and her kind attention, I began to feel human again. That's when I started realizing what my mental condition was. I didn't know the guy I was looking at in the mirror anymore. This guy was gaunt and hollow-looking, inside and out.

Time out: Talking about myself like this sounds more like a plot in a bad novel. I do apologize. I stopped the minute that I realized it myself. But after thinking it over, it's how things were. I was living inside that novel at the time. I can dress it up or explain how I felt and looked.

Bob drove a dark green 1963 split-window Corvette that he kept in mint condition. Bob was a pragmatist. He believed that everything had to be functional and serve a purpose at the same time. His Corvette was useful when dating, but it wasn't practical for anything else. It was especially impractical when it came to driving on snow and ice. So, he decided to trade it for something more practical. The year was 1969, but the new 1970 models were out, and Bob bought a Ford Galaxie 500 Coupe. Dark green, of course. In those days, British Racing Green was all the rage. When he realized what he was being offered for his Corvette was not in line with its condition and desirability, he kept it. He bought the Galaxie outright.

I forgot to mention that, despite being well-to-do, Bob was a tight ass. He came from a prominent family of means back East somewhere. He went to school at an Ivy League College. Daddy owned an art gallery. In other words, he was well-bred, well-educated, and had a lot of money. But Bob's strong suit was that he was still a nice guy. He was good-looking also. The ladies loved Bob no matter which car he drove.

Apparently, I already had a reputation for speaking my mind. It would help you understand people like me if you knew one thing. We are always looking for the enemy hiding around the corner. My shrink calls it hypervigilance. I call it looking for the bad in people. That wouldn't be a problem if people like me could keep our mouths shut, but we can't. Literally, we can't. Whatever is in our minds comes out of our mouths. We don't mean it to sound hateful, but it often does. We can piss people off without trying.

Suppose I went to Rome and attended Easter Mass at the Vatican. In that case, I could be standing in the middle of St. Peter's Square with half a million people around me. When the Pope walked out on the balcony and looked out into the ocean of flesh below, he would look back and ask his Cardinal, "Who let that ass-hole in?" And he would be pointing at me.

I don't mean to do it. It just happens. It's part of my new, altered personality. The new personality that I came home from Vietnam with. Guys that have been there don't notice it. The rest of you notice the hell out of it.

Enough about me. Back to Bob's story. After Bob bought his new Galaxie 500, he took his Corvette to new and used car dealers and offered to sell it. Small dealers who couldn't afford it would tell him it was worth a fortune. The ones that could afford it offered him way less. Bob was getting frustrated. He asked me to come with him and help him sell it.

As I said, Bob was a good guy. I don't know if he was asking me to help or using that as an excuse to get me out of the townhouse. I suspect the latter. At the time, I didn't care. I was ready to go out and I didn't own a car. So, I was happy to ride along.

After four or five stops, we came to Chuck Ruwart Chevrolet. 2555 South Colorado Blvd. At first, a salesman came out and tried to negotiate a price. Bob kept insisting on talking to the used car manager. The used car manager's name was Boots Stallings. I remember that because it was such an unusual name. The salesman finally gave up when he discovered that Bob had bought a car and only wanted to sell his trade. Plus, he acted like he was insulted when Bob told him that he had bought a Ford.

Boots took a few minutes and looked at Bob's Corvette. He started it but didn't drive it. He asked if Bob had the title with him? Bob did. Boots admitted that it was a nice car. Then he went into another long-winded spiel about how his dealership only sold the best and nicest low-mileage Corvettes. It almost sounded like he was going to tell Bob that his car wasn't nice enough to sell on his lot. I think he remembered then that he had already admitted it was a nice car. He mentioned several times that they were the number one used Corvette dealer in Colorado. He corrected himself and widened the focus. They were the largest used Corvette and new Corvette dealer in the five-state area.

This went on for five minutes before Boots promised Bob that his Corvette would only go home with someone who genuinely appreciated its condition and rarity. Bob knew that already. Chevy only made the five-window coupe that one year. Then Boots Stallings offered Bob the lowest price he had been offered for the car.

I don't know why, but that struck me wrong, and I lit into him. I asked him how, in God's name, his dealership ever got to be the largest dealer anywhere when he tried to steal the perfect Corvettes and obviously bought rough ones. I pointed to one next to us that was on the edgy side. I went on for several minutes until Boots finally stopped me. He asked me to wait. He said he wanted to get a second opinion from his manager.

His name was Bert Bangston or something like that. When he came out, I repeated everything that I had said before, plus some. Finally, he reached up, pinched my beard with his forefinger and thumb, and asked me to stop talking. He didn't grab it in an offensive way. He did it in a way that seemed more like he was telling me that he didn't like it, but I stopped talking and listened.

He asked me what I did for a living. I told him I didn't have a job and wasn't looking at the time. He asked if I would consider selling cars. I would have considered anything. I was running out of money again. I said maybe. He told me to shave off my beard and be there at 8 am the following day, and he would give me an office and let me pick out a new car to drive as a demonstrator. The car almost got me, but I said no. I told him I didn't want to shave my beard. He thought for a second and told me to be there at 8 and wear a suit and tie. I told him I didn't own one of those either. That's when Bob broke in. Bob said he would give me some white shirts and ties. He wasn't using them. The general manager said he would be okay with that, but I would have to buy a sports coat as soon as I got paid.

I was employed in a house of thieves, but now, I had a place to live, a job, and a car.

I worked my shift and sold a few cars. But when people I talked to came back later and bought the car that I showed them, I was supposed to get half of the commission if they asked for me. My fellow salesmen didn't see it that way. In those days, you were expected to split the commission between the guy that sold the car and the guy that closed the deal. But again, they didn't see it that way.

As the days passed, it happened more often. Then, a customer confirmed what I knew was happening. He thanked me for selling him his new car. He told me that he loved it. Then he said, "I asked for you, and your buddy told me you worked together. He said he would write it up for you. He said that you would get the credit for the sale. He did do that, didn't he?"

I was selling cars like crazy, but I wasn't getting paid. I was starting to realize that I had to work both shifts to keep my "buddies" from stealing my customers. And I was beginning to realize that this Chevrolet dealer wasn't as good as Boots had told me it was. The service department sucked. New cars were washed and put on the lot without inspections. Factory oversights and mistakes were fixed when the customer returned the truck or car and complained. My dealer was getting paid to do a presale service, and he wasn't doing it. Then, he was getting paid customer labor rates to fix what he should have caught in the pre-service inspection. As a result, he had a bunch of unhappy customers. The salespeople weren't any better. They hid when they saw a car that they sold coming in for service.

Don't ask me why, but I had scruples. I was determined to sell cars the right way.

During my third week as a car salesman, this good-looking, very naïve young lady came in looking for a new Malibu. I showed her what we had. There were plenty, but I could see that she needed guidance. After she said she didn't like the Malibu, I suggested she look at the Buick Skylark. I liked Buicks. My shift was over, and I knew a Buick dealership was just down the road from where I lived. So, I suggested I go with her and help her look at the Skylarks. I drove my Chevy demo, and she drove her car. It didn't go unnoticed that I drove up in a car with a dealer plate on it.

No one said anything until she bought the Skylark, and I handled the negotiations. The owner's son was the general sales manager. He came in and asked why I was helping a competitor sell a car and not selling her a Chevy.

I asked him to take my offer, and then we would talk. So he did, she did, and I did. Then I explained my situation and that I was unhappy selling Chevrolets, and he hired me.

Here's the thing. Back then, you could either sink or swim selling cars. There wasn't any training. No one taught you how to sell a car or close a deal. It was "on-the-job" training at its finest. You either learned to sell cars, or you starved to death. Only making minimum wage was frowned on. If you got minimum wage, you didn't sell any cars. They weren't letting me drive a brand-new Buick LeSabre just for shits and giggles. A demo was part of my pay plan. They even gave me ten gallons of gas each month to cover customer demo rides in my LeSabre. They often loaned demos to unhappy customers while they waited for the service department to repair their cars.

I wasn't starving. I made enough money to get my own apartment. It was less than a mile from work and cut my rent in half, but it wasn't free. I still had to pay rent and buy food. I didn't have much left to entertain myself, much less the ladies. I did go on a date occasionally. Not often, but sometimes.

I was separated, so why not. This time, I was taking Brenda at her word. She told me not to return in three days and try to talk her into letting me come home. I think she meant it. Plus, she did say that she didn't want me to be around the kids.

My dates usually ended an hour after they started. I wasn't rude or anything like that. I just wasn't in the mood for the "dating scene." I usually had a few drinks alone or with my new friend from work, Jerry Larimer.

Jerry was a good guy. He drank too much, but we all did back then. No one frowned on it. If you got caught driving drunk, the policeman would usually ask what was happening and let you talk a little. If you didn't give him a ration of crap, most of them would ensure you got home okay and then take your keys. If you were smart, you could usually talk them into leaving your keys with a friend or, in my case, my landlord. But, if you were knee-walking, commode-hugging drunk, and rude, you would spend the night in jail.

There weren't as many "social norms" in those days. Good or bad, cops didn't hassle people just to screw with them. Most of them, at least in Colorado, were good guys. I got more than one break from the police back then. Don't misunderstand. I wasn't a rabble-rouser, but everyone drove a little faster when the streets were empty late at night. Not just me, everybody. When the sign said thirty-five, it meant forty-five or fifty if it was past midnight and the streets were empty. No big deal, even if you were pulled over, it wasn't a big deal. Most of Denver and the surrounding towns had at least four-lane streets.

Here, I'll tell you a story that will help you understand. This was later and not in the timeline I am working on, but it is close enough and makes my point.

John Helzer was single and good-looking. Not to me, but the girls liked him. He drank and played a lot. John loved fast boats and cars. Toys, in general. He lived at home and had no overhead. He spent his money on toys. He had a snowmobile, a Chris-Craft mahogany wooden powerboat that I would have killed to own. His toys were pristine. He took care of them.

John talked our General Manager into letting him drive a Buick Skylark GS 455 Stage 1 as his demo. Helzer gave sound reasoning when he made his pitch. First, it would probably sell within a week or two after he took it, so it wouldn't be a slow mover like the other demos. They sold at the list price, so it wouldn't cost the dealer as much as the other demos. Most demos were sold at cost when they miled out as a demo.

Then John hit the G.M. where it hurt, in the pocketbook. It was good advertising. Most people would never see this car. Very few people back then knew this, but it was the fastest car you could buy stock. And it was a good-looking car. It had looks and power. They were faster than the Hemi six-packs by a fraction but faster. Faster than the GTO by a second or more in a quarter mile. This same engine was used in the police interceptor vehicles used by almost all undercover agents and a bunch of CHP vehicles. You couldn't outrun them. A Denver undercover cop was clocked at 140 mph on I-25 by a Colorado highway patrol officer. The undercover cop was driving a plain-Jane black two-door LeSabre coupe that was special ordered. Hell, it had dog dishes in place of the stock full-wheel covers. They let the undercover agent buy it because he was too big to sit in the smaller cars they usually drove. 140 mph in a full-sized sedan.

Helzer would head down to the Pittsburg Plate Glass Company parking lot every Saturday night, where the local drag racing nuts hung out. Half of them drove Mopar's. PPG had a side road that was about a half-mile long and closed off at both ends. The street was paved by PPG and was for their use. It was not a city street. There was no traffic around it.

All the drag racers met there on Saturdays and raced right downtown. They even got brave enough to set up a "Christmas tree" to start the race and an electric timer to time each race. Of course, the police watched to make sure no one got crazy. But they did it from the Sixth Avenue bridge up above PPG. They would rather have it happen where it was safe, and they could monitor it than on a different neighborhood side street every night. I never heard of anyone getting hurt there. A crapload of engines and transmissions blew up, but no one got hurt.

That's the difference between then and now. Cops and people used common sense. It was an excellent time to be alive if you were hard-working and honest. Even if you didn't make a lot of money, there were still things you could do.

Buick didn't advertise their cars as muscle cars like Chevy and Pontiac did. It didn't fit the image they were trying to project. Buicks were the cars that professionals drove, Doctors, and businessmen. Wealthy housewives were their target owners.

It was still 1970. Vietnam was the main topic of the news. Walter Cronkite was still telling how it was. Riots and crazy people were coming out of the woodwork in other parts of the country. But Colorado was still Colorado, and Denver was still called "Cow Town." The biggest crowds were still at the Coliseum when the Stock Show was in town.

I still hadn't told anyone at work that I served in Vietnam. I never mentioned that I was an officer.

Near the end of that Summer, when Fall was close, evenings were cold and nippy. I took an "up" that I wouldn't have taken if we were busy. (Ups were what we called customers.) You could always tell when a "flake" walked on the lot. Every salesman in the store decided to go to the bathroom at the same time. You couldn't find a salesman if your life depended on it. I was the last to notice the guy and my sales manager was watching. So, I walked out and talked to him.

On the way out, I saw what this guy was driving. He was in an old pickup that looked like it had been beaten to hell. Even from the showroom, I could see what it was. It smoked. There wasn't a straight panel on it anywhere. The hood had smoke, or steam, coming up from the back next to the windshield. I notice the headliner. It was hanging down around the rear-view mirror. The windshield was cracked on both sides. There were two categories that a truck, or car, this bad fit into.

There wasn't anything good that I could say about this guy's trade-in except that it wouldn't take long to appraise it. My used car manager usually just looked out his window and wrote "weigh it" on the appraisal slip. Then, in pencil down at the bottom, he wrote $25.

For vehicles he didn't want at any price, he wrote "POS." (Piece of shiest, as my owner calls them. He was German.) They were the trades that came in on a hook. Or looked like this guy's trade.

Any money you gave a customer for a trade like this one was a discount on the price of the new vehicle. One of my favorite closes was when a customer turned down what you were offering him for his trade. Especially, if he asked for more, was…. "What if I gave you $500 to keep your trade-in?" You only used that one when you already knew it was over and wanted the guy to leave. But sometimes, it woke them up, and they kept their trade and bought your car. This guy looked like one of those customers, except I doubted he could come up with a down payment without his trade. He looked that bad.

I walked out, shook his hand, and welcomed him to our store. "Welcome to Bill Dreiling Buick. My name is Ben Speed. And your name is?"

"I'm John Johnson. I drove down from Central City, and I'm looking for a good used truck."

Epilogue:

At the time I wrote this book, USA Today reported that 22 American veterans commit suicide every day. The Veterans Administration guesses that it is more like 18 per day. Those numbers do not include deaths from alcoholism or injuries that occurred during combat and later resulted in death. It didn't include diseases related to exposure to Agent Orange and the other defoliants used during the Vietnam War. It didn't include diseases like diabetes and a myriad of individual cancers caused by Agent Orange or the fumes from burning jet fuel and out-house shit. That is how the military got rid of human waste at the time.

It has been more than 40 years since the end of the war in Vietnam. Several reports that I've found online suggest that there have been more Vietnam veterans who died by their own hands than died in combat. More than 50,000 names are on the "Wall" in Washington, D.C.

PTSD is considered the prime reason for these numbers.

PTSD is not peculiar to Vietnam Veterans. The number of suicides has not dropped as we Vietnam Vets age out. We're being replaced by Veterans from the Middle East Wars, the Gulf Wars, and Afghanistan conflicts. By the way, conflict is just another word for war. But you know that.

If, after reading this, you think that I am a pacifist, you are wrong. I believe wars are inevitable, and we should be ready to fight them.

I believe that the best way to avoid war is to be the biggest and baddest dog in town. I believe in being the owner of the dog that no one wants to mess with, and I believe in keeping him by my side. I also think that the price for this kind of security is high. Mentally and physically. I still say it's worth it.

I just thought you should know.

****

P.S. I'm not superstitious, but just in case, one of my readers is. I never use any numbers between twelve and fourteen in my books. If you suffer from the dreaded triskaidekaphobia, you can thank me later.

This was the first book that I attempted to write. I am dyslexic. I've never read a book myself. But I'm not a heathen. I've listened to hundreds of books on CD. Plus, this is the twelfth book that I have written. I had considered all of them practice for when I decided to finish this one.

I write the Sonny Walters, P.I. Case Study series. The first couple were good stories but not written very well. I was learning. They are still worth reading, but I'm a little biased. "Rated R for Violence" was the first book I wrote using writing aids. Spell Check and later Grammarly. It was a little better and had a great storyline… in fact, two different storylines. It was a double case study—two books for the price of one.

I used my computer's "Read Aloud" program and Grammarly in the last few books I have written. So I can hear my words as I write them. I hope it makes them even more readable and enjoyable.

There have been nine books in the Sonny Walters series. The last one is one of my favorites. "The Naughty Professor Case." It might be a little edgy for some of you. But it's more the topic than the writing that makes it edgy. So go ahead and read it. It won't kill you. "Dog Gone Wife" runs a close second in my favorites.

I have written two "G" rated books for my relatives, grandkids, and close friends. There's nary a foul word in them... clean topics, written with my friends and family in mind. Follow the adventures of Bartholomew Reese, or Bat Reese, as his friends call him, in "Batteries."

On a totally different path is "Village of the Bison Hunters." It follows an ancient prehistoric family searching for a village where they can live in peace. But, unfortunately, in the beginning, peace is the last thing they find.

Thanks for supporting a disabled Veteran and buying this book. I do appreciate it. I hope you enjoyed reading it. If you did, let your friends know. I always appreciate finding new readers. If you don't, let me know. Email me at.

Thank you again,
Ben Speed

Dedication:

This book is dedicated to the ladies in my life. Miriam, my mother, for giving me life. Brenda, for giving me two beautiful children. Robin, for teaching me humility. Jodie, for teaching me how ladies act. Ivy, for giving me grandchildren that I can be proud of. Last but not least, for my wife, Charlene, for sticking with me even when I fall off the deep end. Without Charlene, I would have drowned years ago.

Made in the USA
Coppell, TX
09 July 2025

51617054R00118